ZEN DOGS:

Drawing Zen Doodle Dogs

By Jane McKenty

Copyright©2015 Jane McKenty

Table of Contents

Disclaimer

While all attempts have been made to verify the information provided in this book, the author does assume any responsibility for errors, omissions, or contrary interpretations of the subject matter contained within. **The information provided in this book is for educational and entertainment purposes only. The reader is responsible for his or her own actions and the author does not accept any responsibilities for any liabilities or damages, real or perceived, resulting from the use of this information.**

The trademarks that are used are without any consent, and the publication of the trademark is without permission or backing by the trademark owner. All trademarks and brands within this book are for clarifying purposes only and are the owned by the owners themselves, not affiliated with this document.

Introduction

The biggest advantage of the book "Zen Dogs: Drawing Zen Doodle Dogs" in relation to other books dealing with similar or the same topic are very detailed instructions accompanied by lots of drawings. I personally believe that theoretical instruction worth very little and are tiring, at least when it comes to the art of drawing or painting. In the drawing, more than anything in the world, counts a motto "Show me and teach me!" Looking at the drawings presented in this book, you will easily be able to draw Zen doodle dogs. The point is that this book is rather a picture book than a text book and I guess that is what is important to you.

If you decide to go into this Zen doodle adventure, you will not only learn how to draw dogs, but you will be familiar with numerous Zen patterns from Zen art of drawing, that you can use for other forms of artistic expressions. In the book "Zen Dogs," there are presented five breeds of dogs through six chapters, in which you will find in detail how to draw Maltese, Chihuahua ... So this book is both for those who love small cute dogs and for fans of "dangerous" dogs like a Bulldog.

Zen drawing can be used for relaxing the brain from busy everyday life, scrapbooks, but also for real works of art. Imagine a drawing or a picture of your favorite breed drawn / painted by your own hand! As it can be an artistic hobby, Zen drawing art can also become a business for those who are interested in it. Let's begin our adventure by drawing Zen Maltese! Keep calm and do the Zen doodle dogs!

Chapter 1-Zen Maltese

Maltese are cute and smart little dogs with white hair. People even call them "Lounge dogs" and they are ideal for those who have problems with dog hairs because they do not have a so-called undercoat. Although slightly built, they are not toys for children still they nicely match with kids and like to walk around and chase balls. Let's draw a cute little Maltese!

The official Zen tile is a square with 9 centimeters long sides, within which are formed Zen drawings and patterns. However, you should not confine your drawings to that dimensions, but you can choose a bigger paper or even a smaller one if you wish your drawing to be tiny.

We will start, of course, by drawing a figure, and while doing that, you should pay special attention to drawing his long hair. The first figure below shows the whole figure of Maltese, that is how he should look in general. At the other pictures below, you can see specific parts of his figure that you should pay attention to, such as his legs, head and tail. As you can see, he has this cute little bow so his hair could not prevent him from seeing.

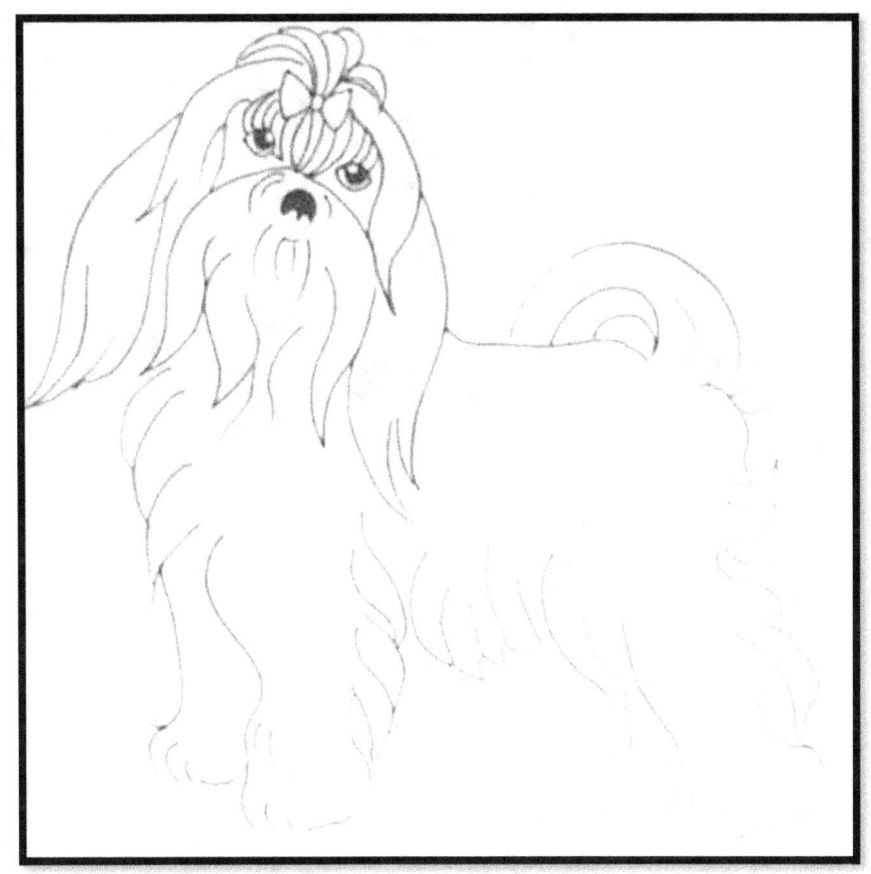

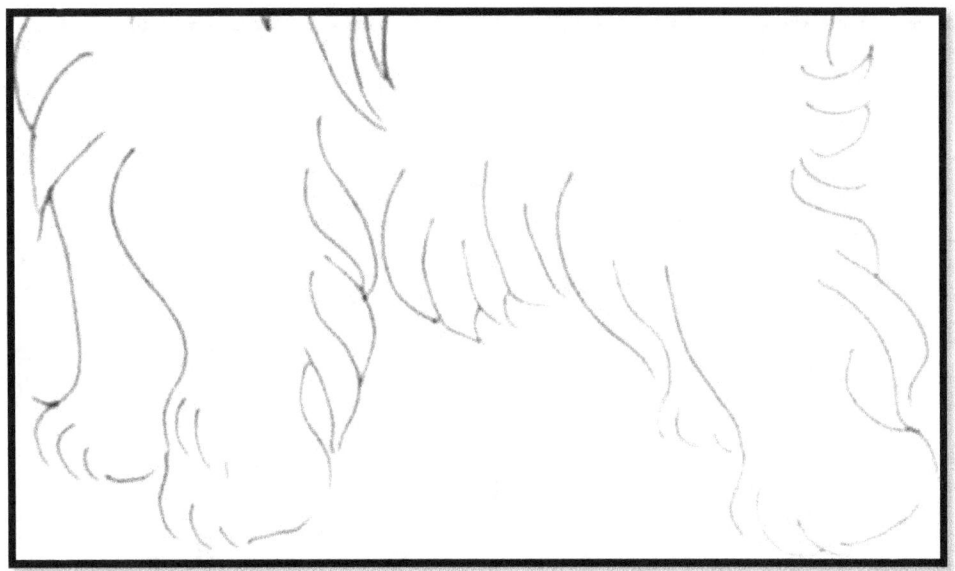

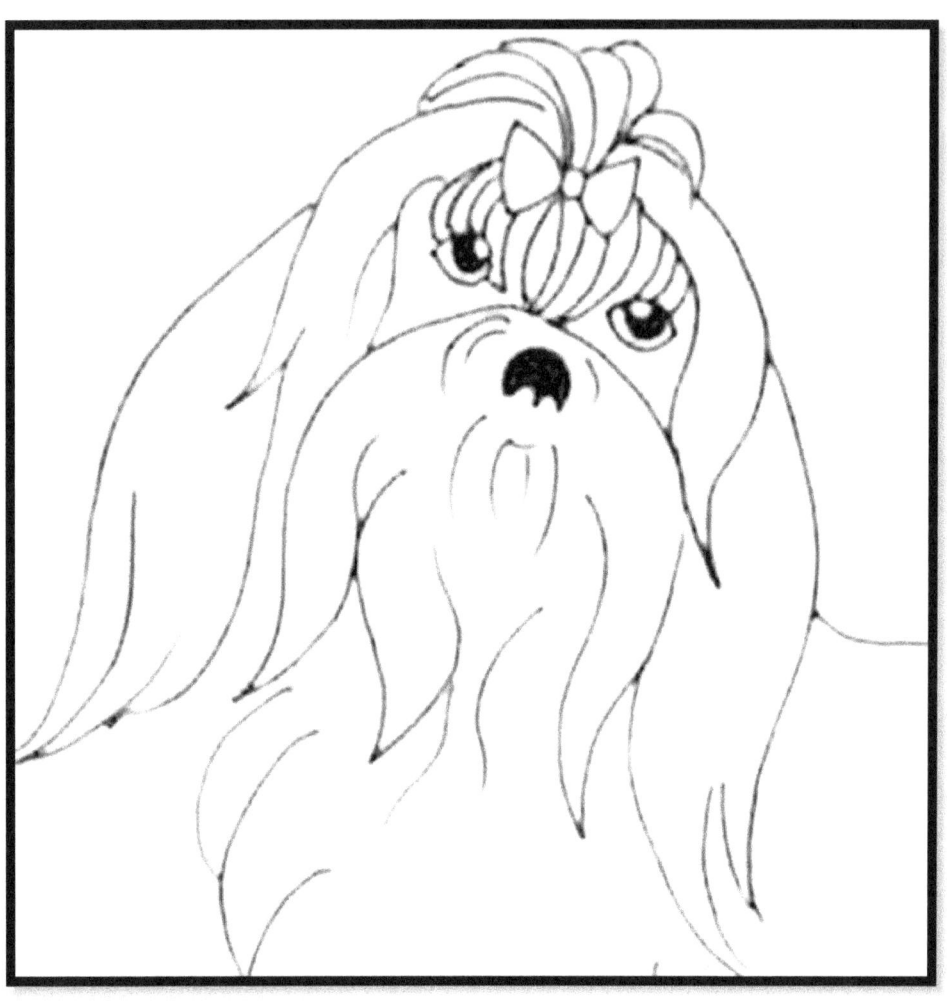

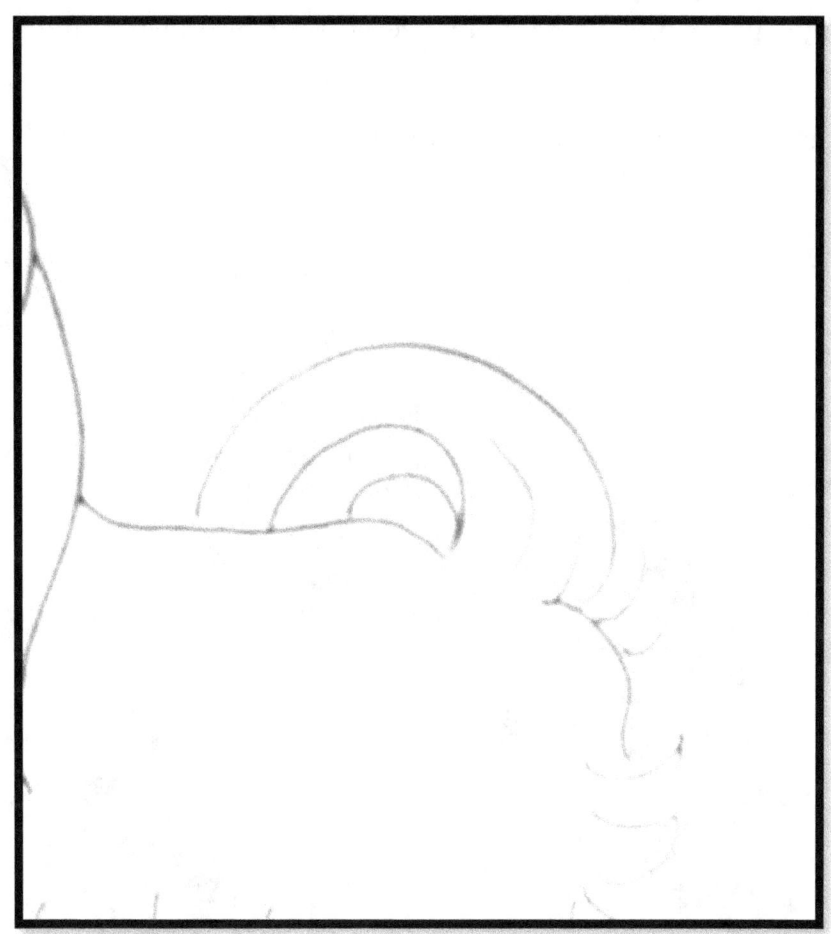

Now, when we managed to form the base of our Zen Maltese, we'll start drawing Zen patterns within the created form. Arm yourself with patience because we do not want to destroy what we have drawn so far. It is best for you to take a thin black marker or, if you are not sure that you will not make a mistake, first draw patterns with ordinary graphite pencil.

We will start from his head, precisely his long ears and a small forehead. On the first drawing below, you can see the patterns I have used for the mentioned parts of his head. It is nothing complex, but if you don`t pay attention, you will easily make a mistake.

On the right picture below, you can see how I have started filling out his long hair with vertical and a bit curved lines. I made sections by drawing some of the lines with a thicker black marker.

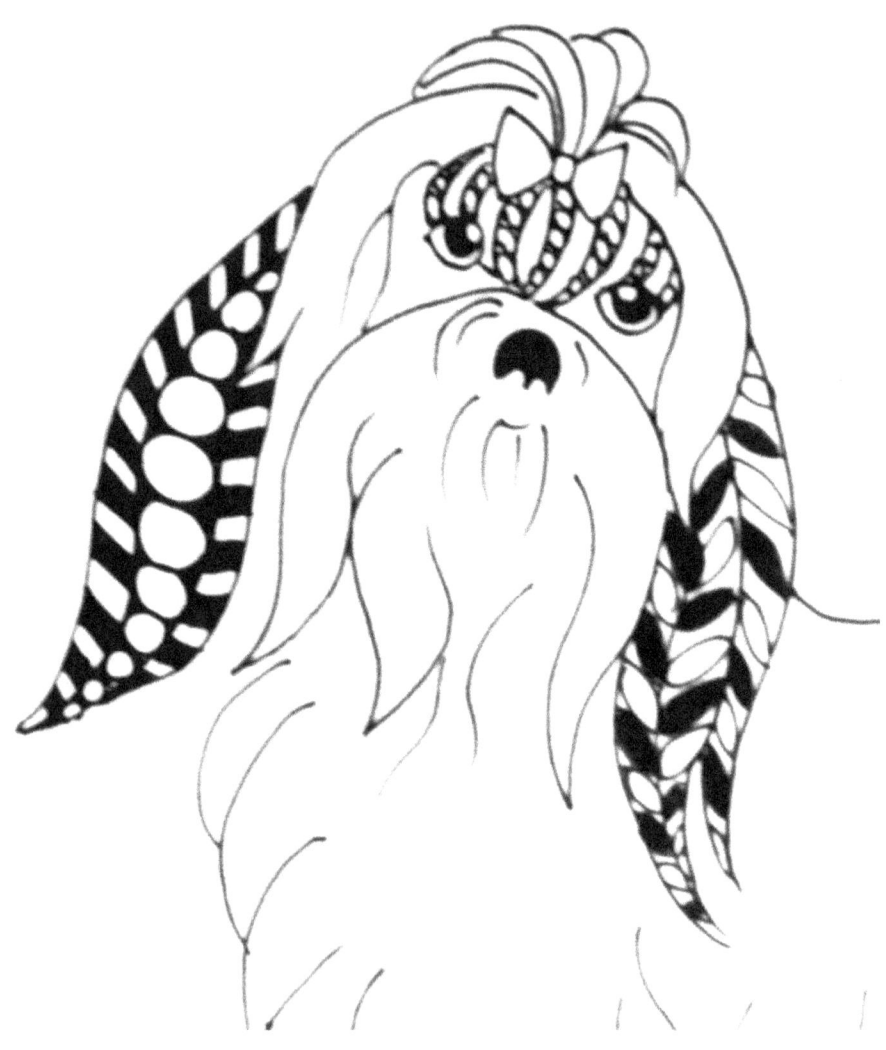

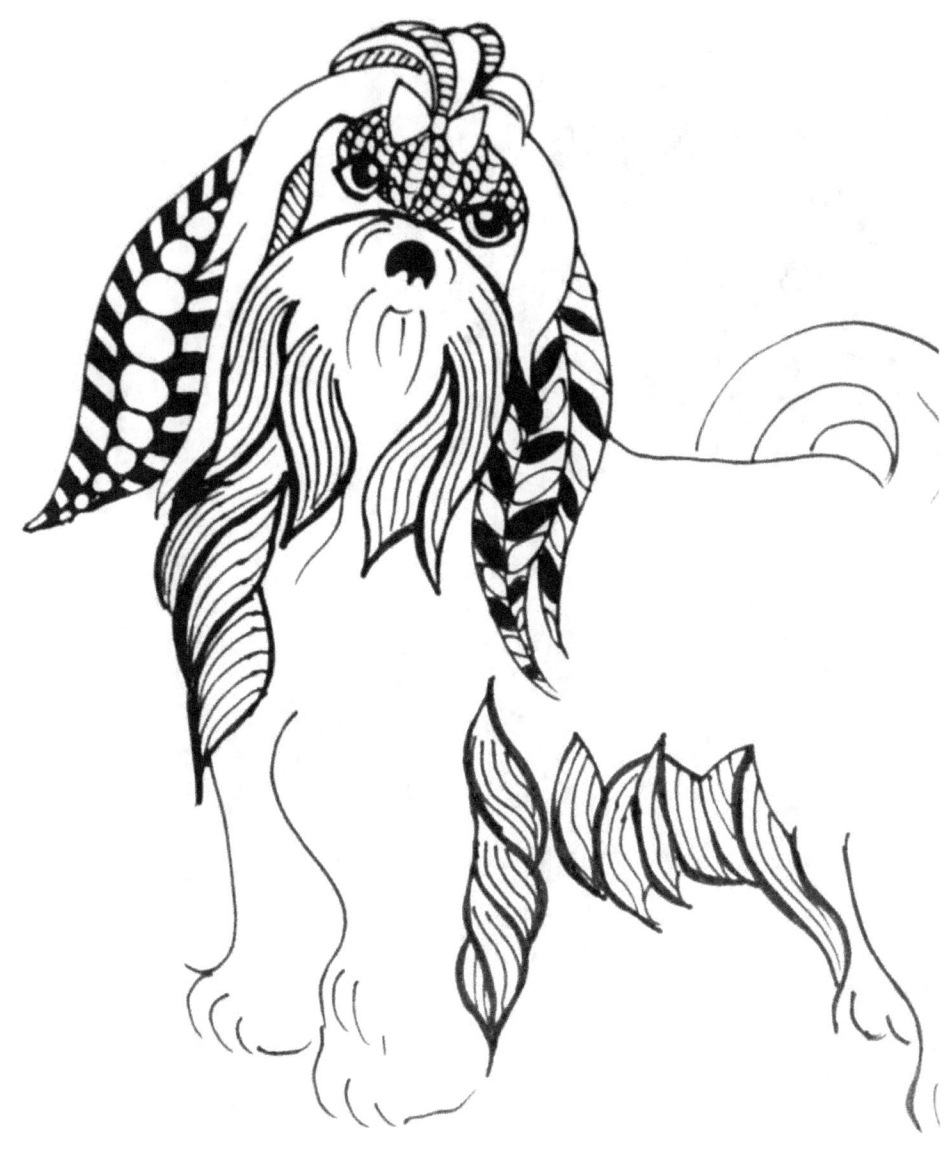

Let`s now look at the whole drawing after we added some empty dots between his face and ears and after filling out his tail with semicircles.

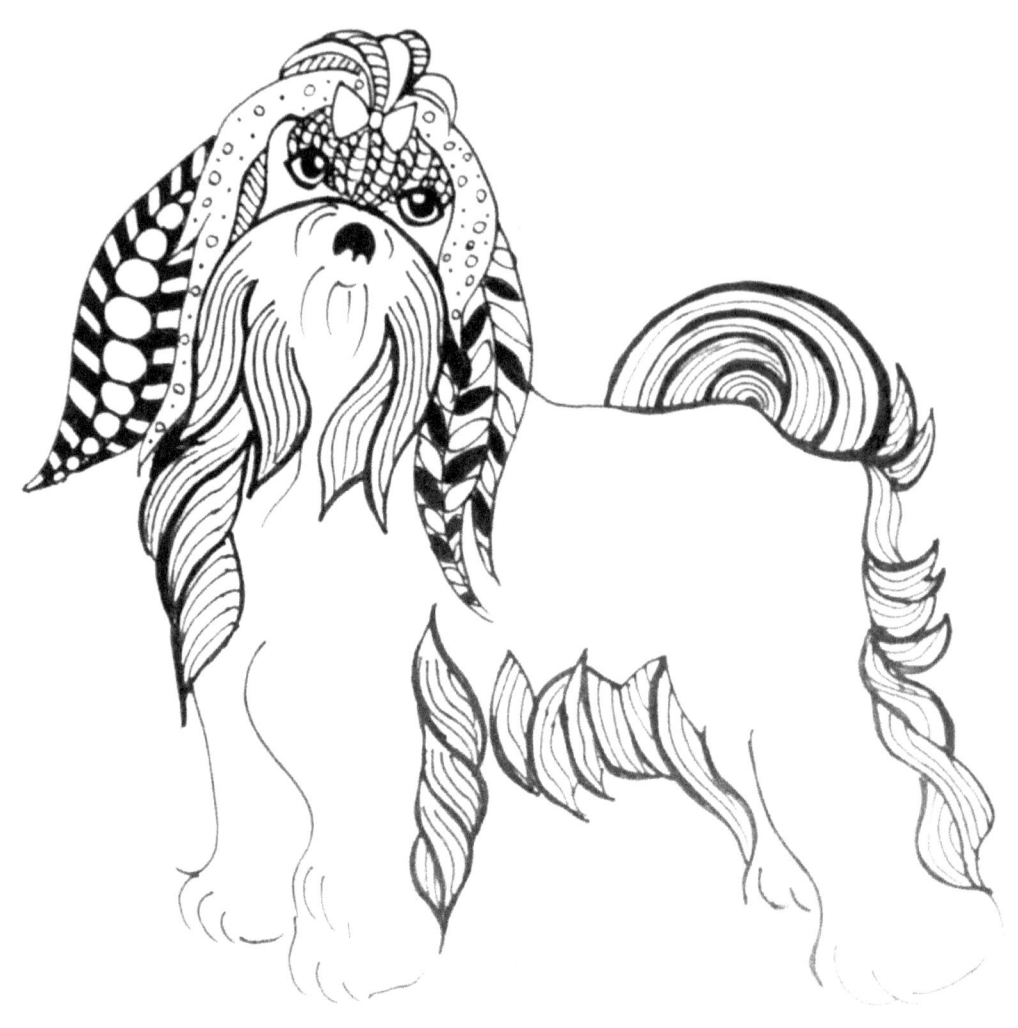

Isn`t it a cute, little dog?!

We will now draw a very beautiful pattern on his back. The picture below on the left shows the whole Maltese and the picture on the right that awesome pattern I am talking about, only enlarged so you can copy it easily.

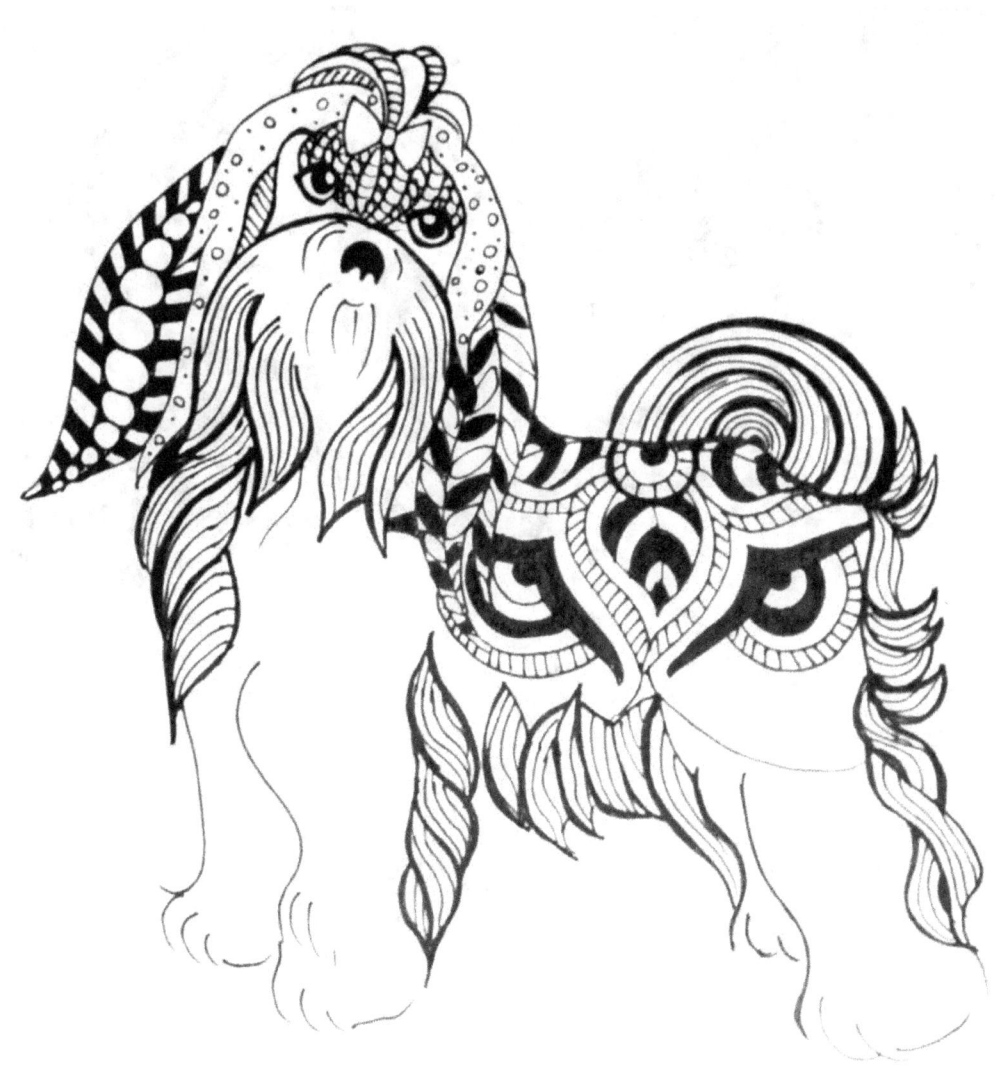

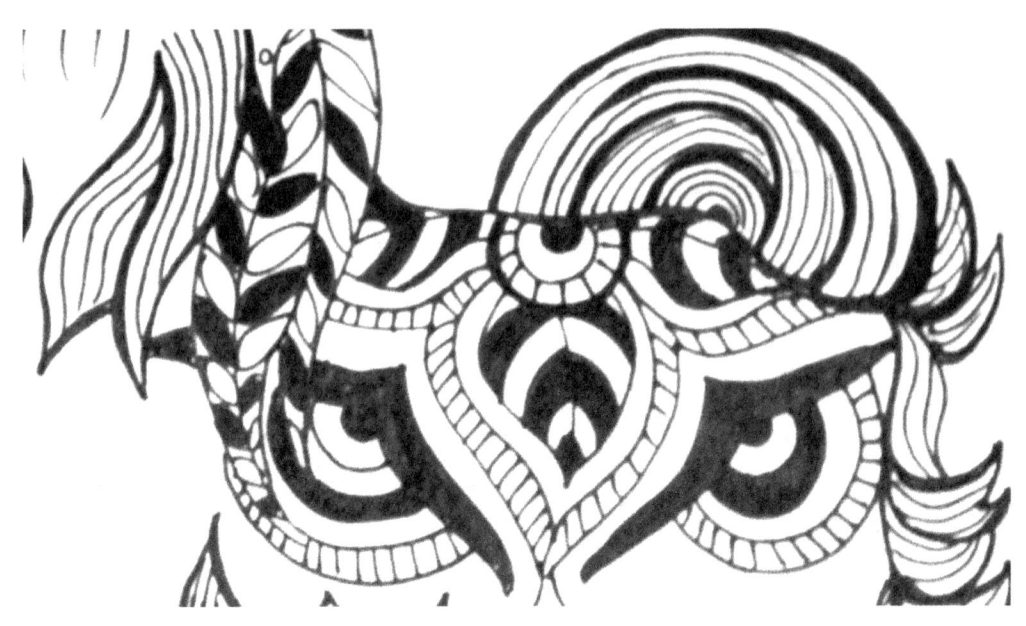

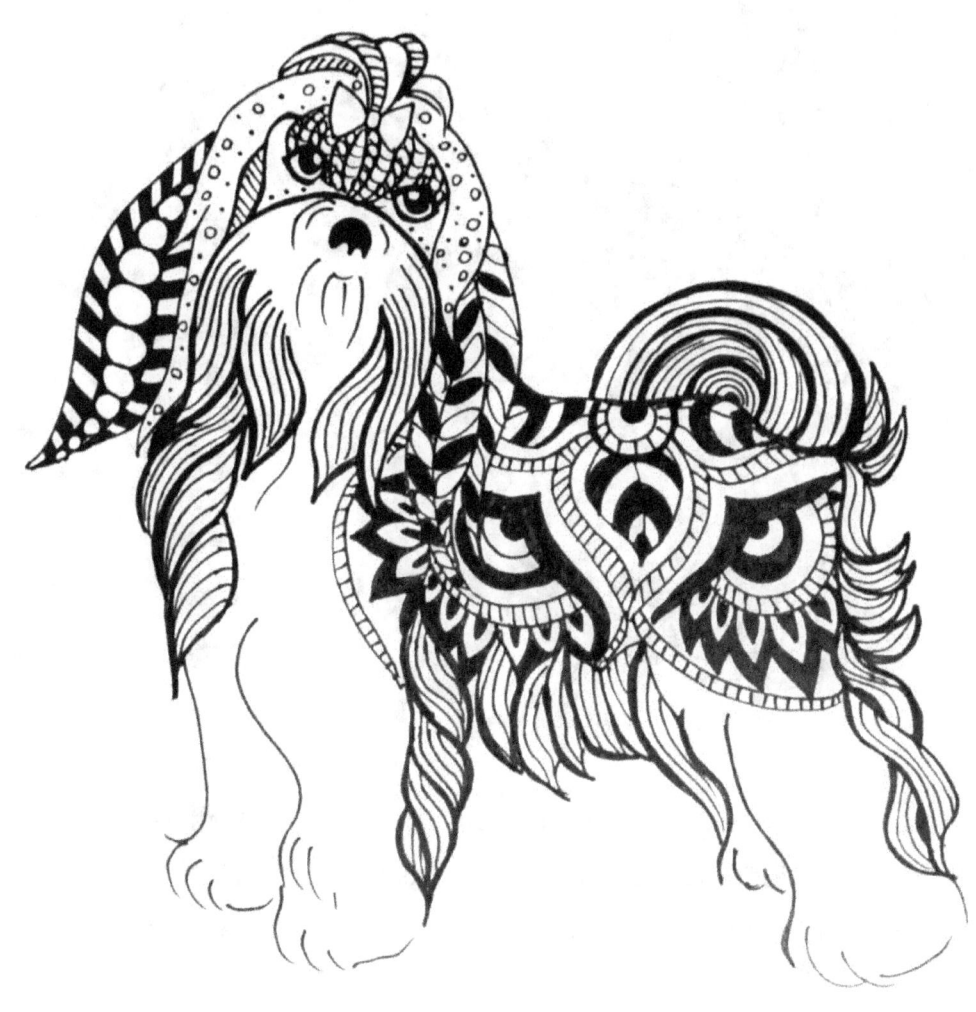

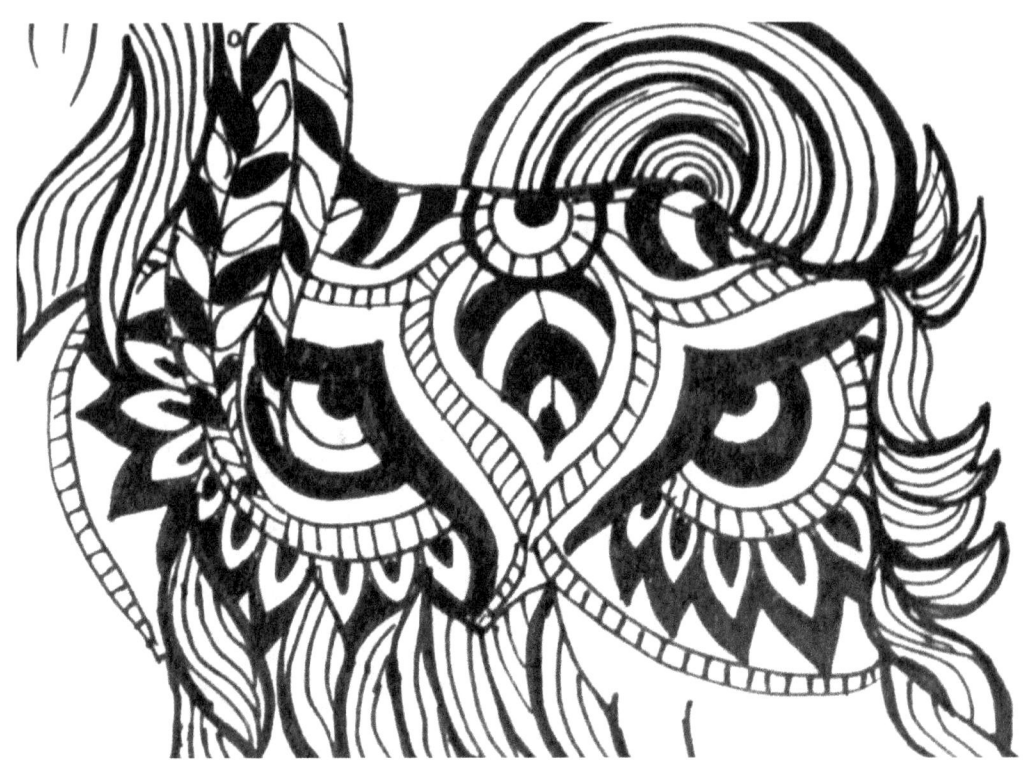

We will now connect, in a way, this nice pattern on Maltese`s back, that looks like his jacket, with line patterns on his long hair. The bond will be in a form of cute little petals as you can see on the left picture and more detailed on the picture below.

Eventually, our small hairy dog will look at the end as shown on the picture on the left. Below you can more closely see the Zen doodles on his legs and his chest.

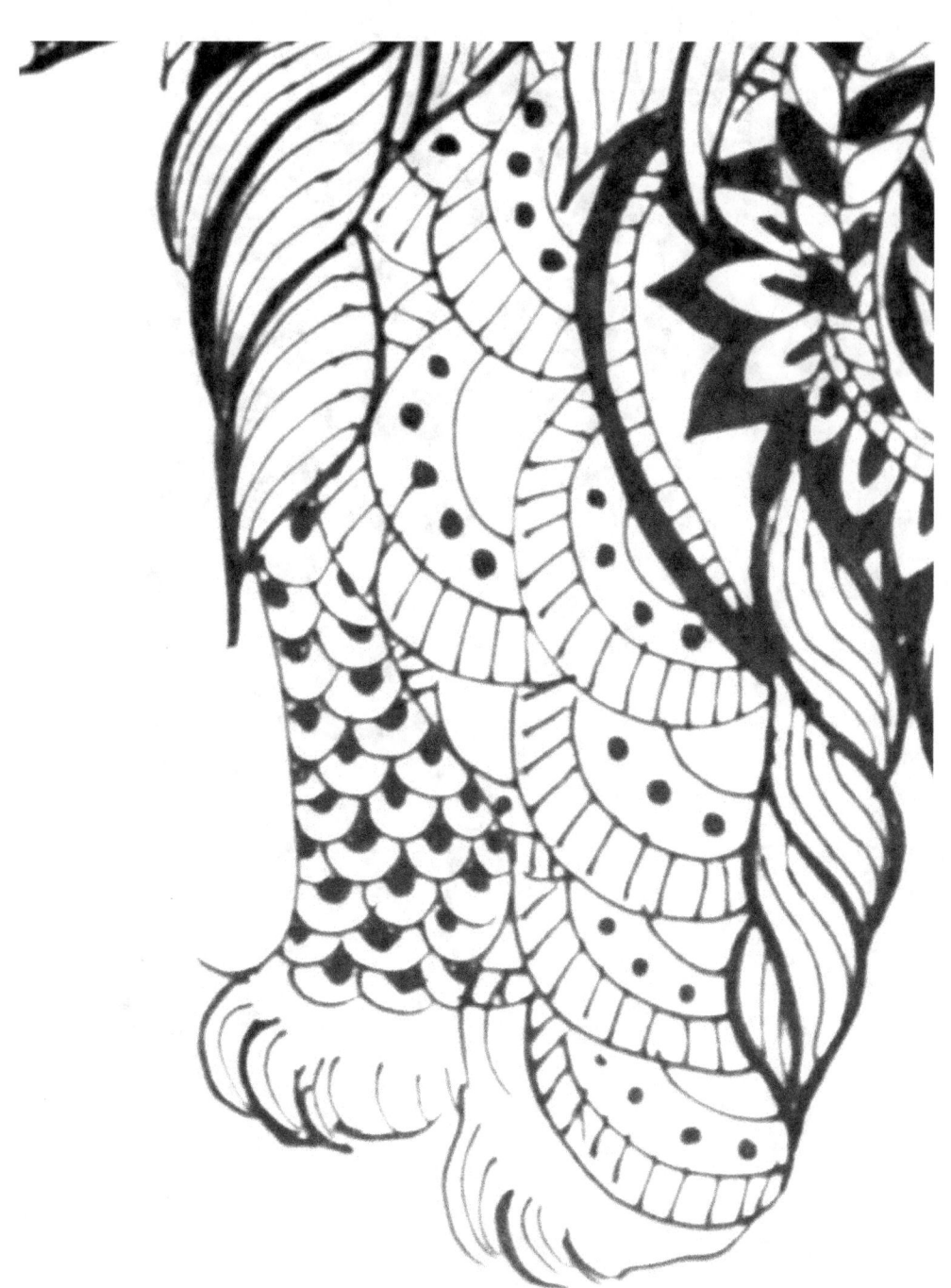

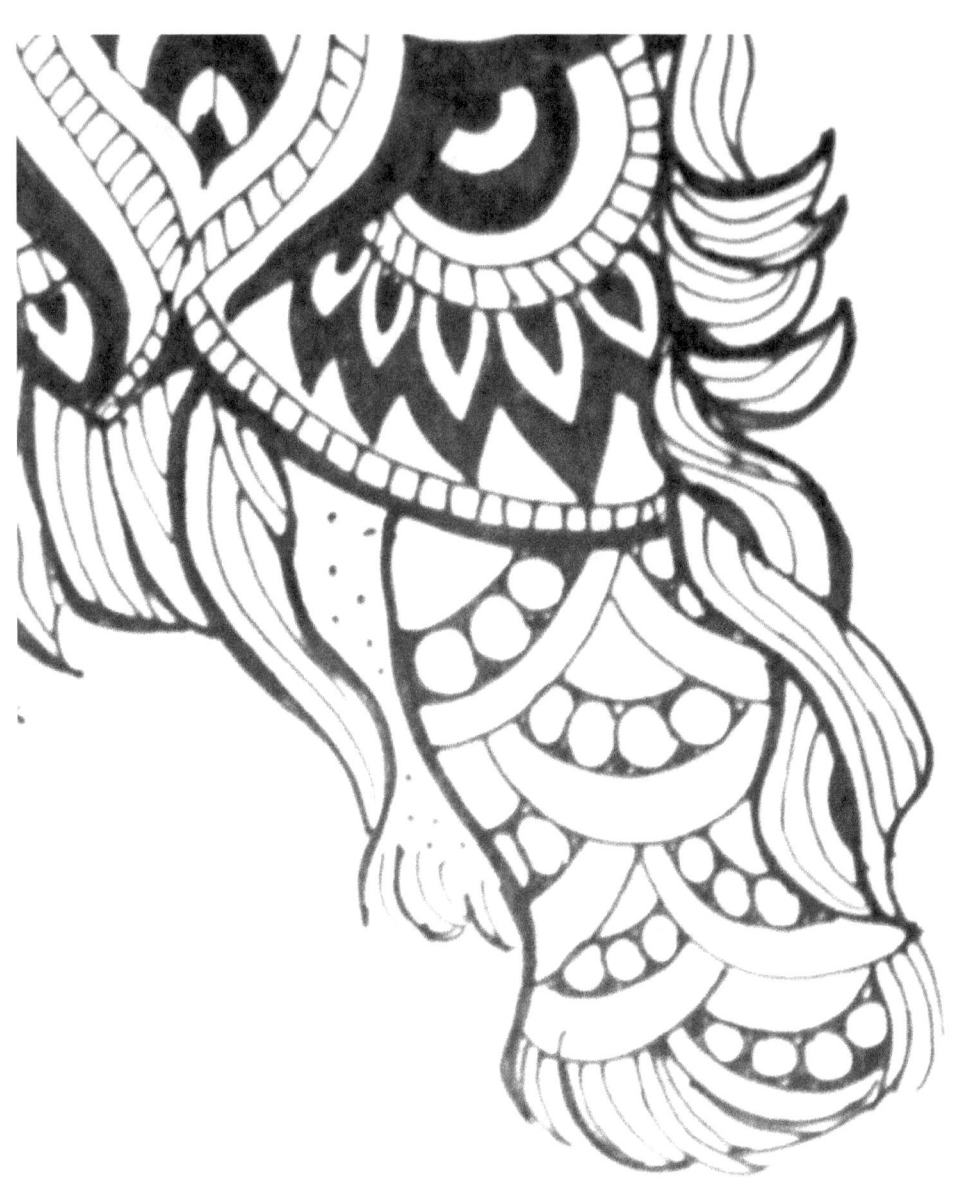

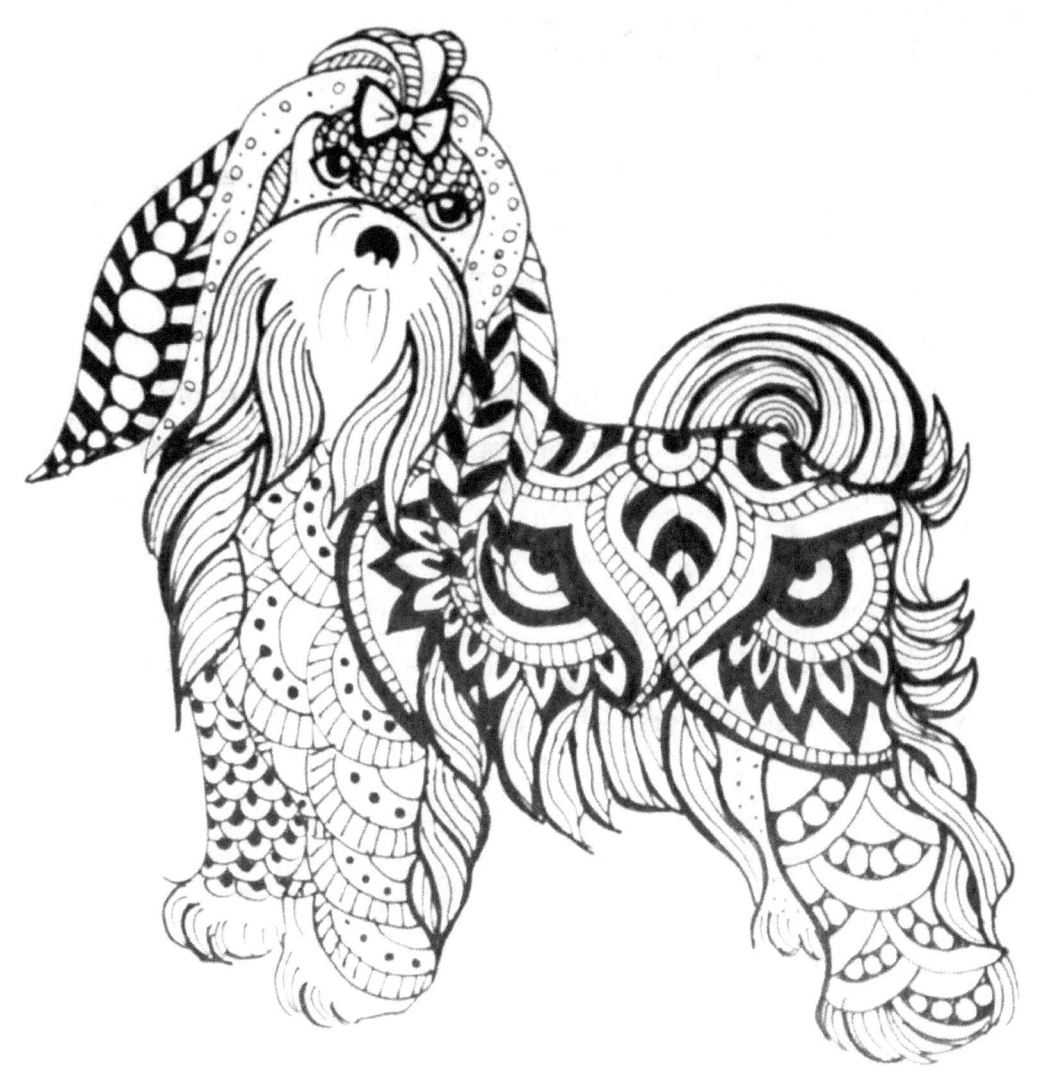

Now, we can move on to our next Zen doodle dog, and it will be a Chihuahua!

Chapter 2- Zen Chihuahua

You have to admit that these little dogs are very cute although large spitfires. Chihuahuas can be considered as dogs "for the lap and cuddling" as they simply enjoy being with their owners. Their hearing is s very sharp and barking loud and shrill. They are known for scaring the burglars and alerting owners when there is a fire or other danger. The popularity of Chihuahuas has increased since the race became a star of Taco Bell commercials - "Yo Quiero Taco Bell."

We will began our drawing by carefully forming the basic shape of Chihuahua`s little, thin body. As you can see their eyes and snout are as usually very black. Do not forget their tiny claws!

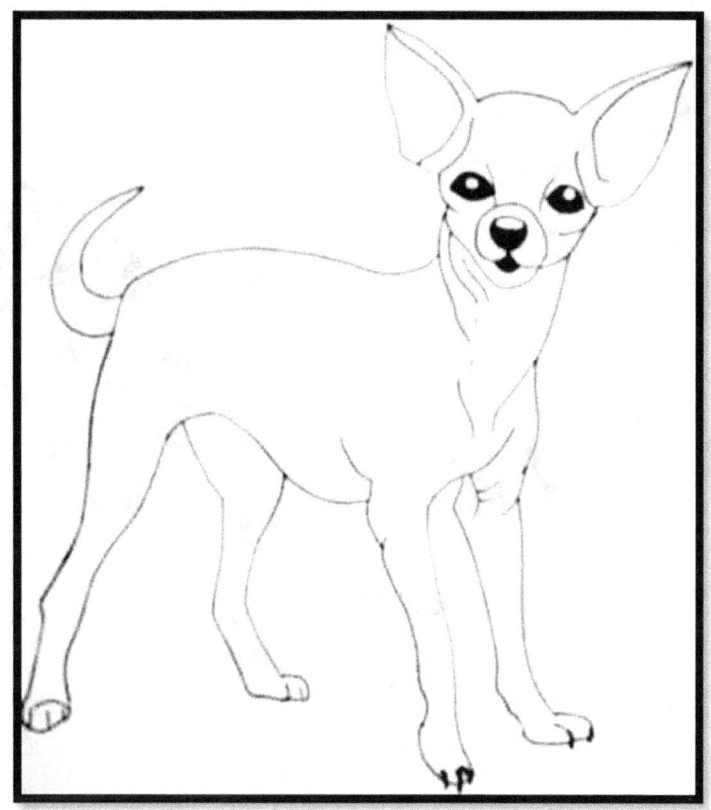

Since the inside of their ears is rather large and visible, as well as their forehead, we can begin to Zen doodle right in those areas, as shown on the pictures below, on the next page.

The more the pattern is tangled, the more benefits to your practice of clearing the mind and creating an engaging Zen drawing. So, once again, be patient and watch your steps!

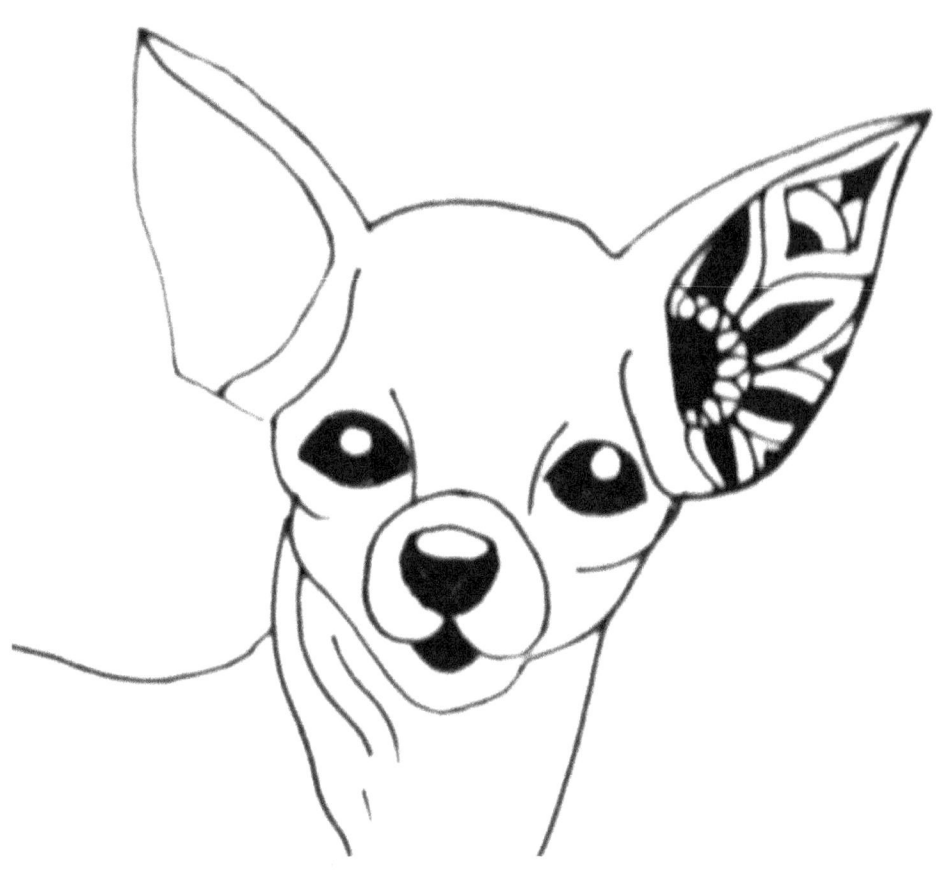

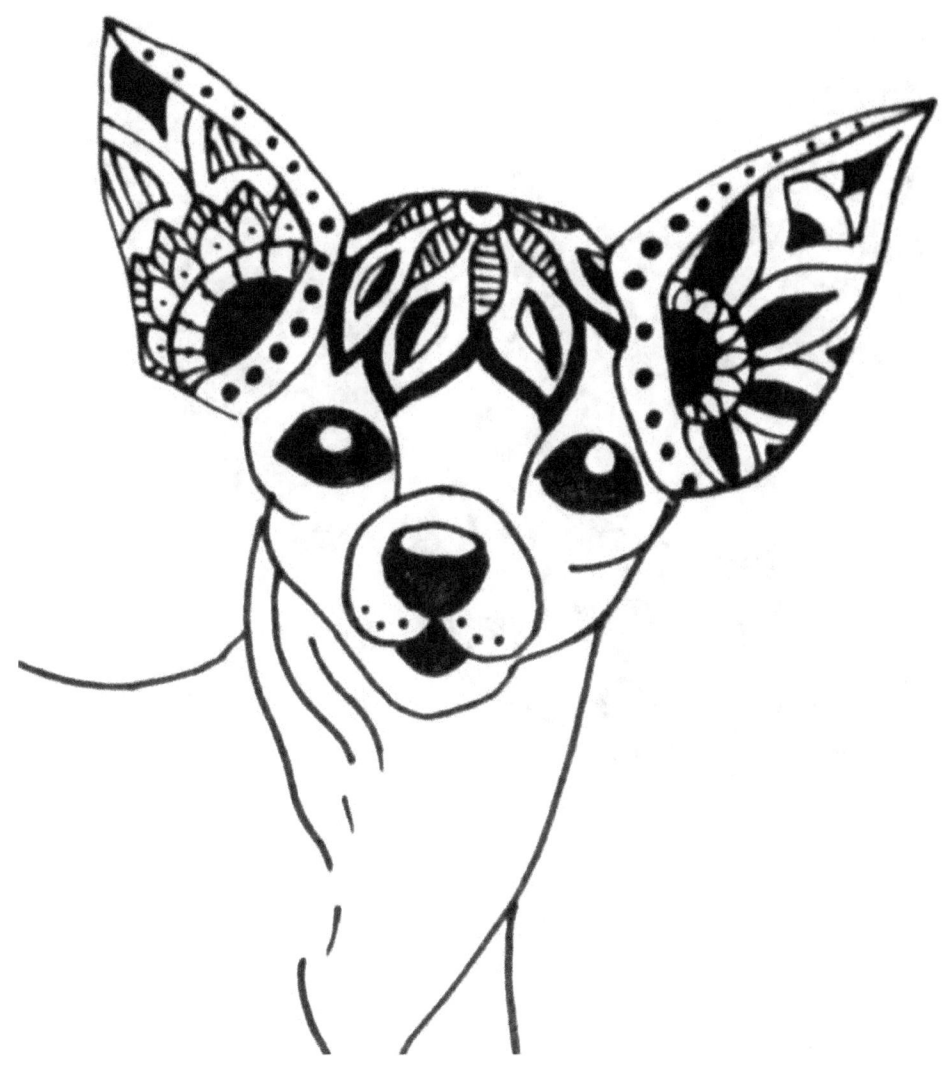

After we finish Chihuahua`s head, we will move on her back by forming rather simple shapes at first shown on the second drawing below.

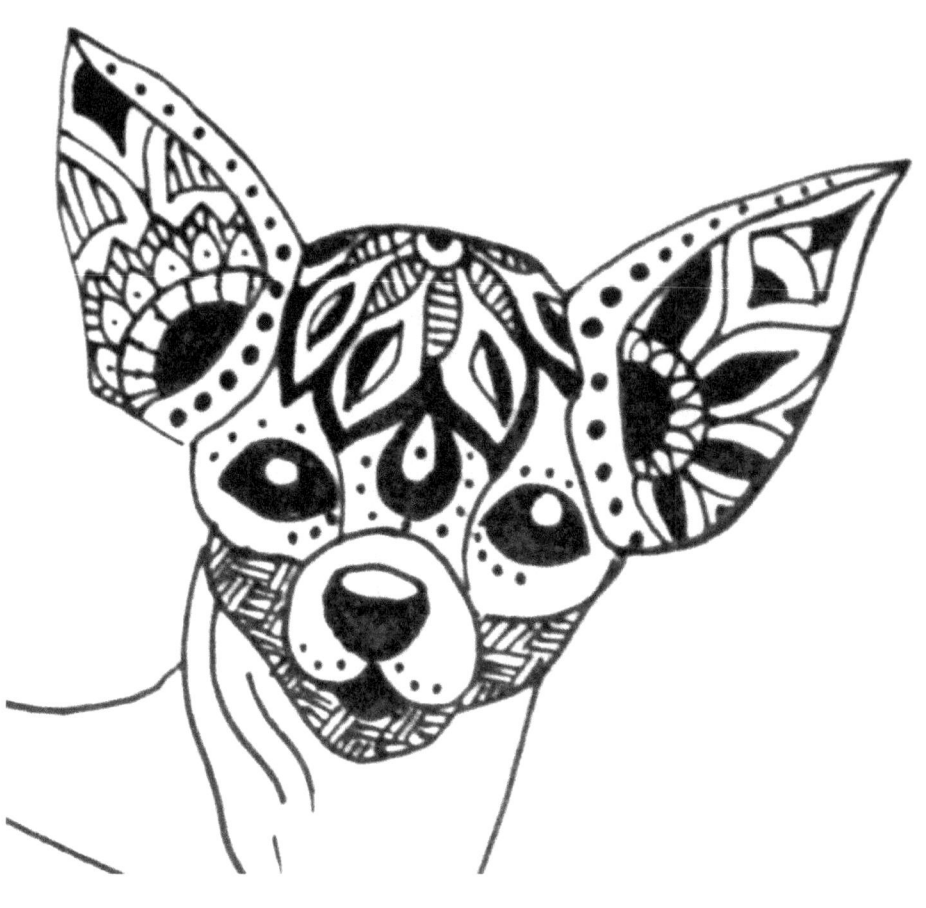

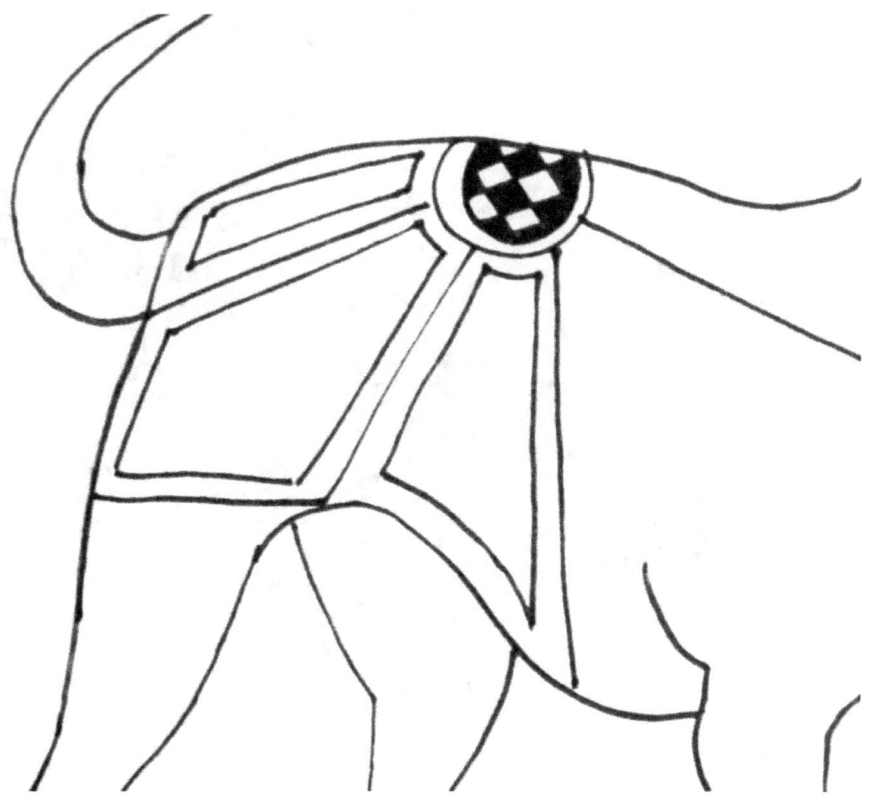

First drawing below shows how our Chihuahua`s back should look like after we add some Zen tangled patterns and the second picture below shows those same Zen doodles zoomed for you to copy it easier. As you can see, we have five different sections and a sixth in the middle in a form of an unfinished circle.

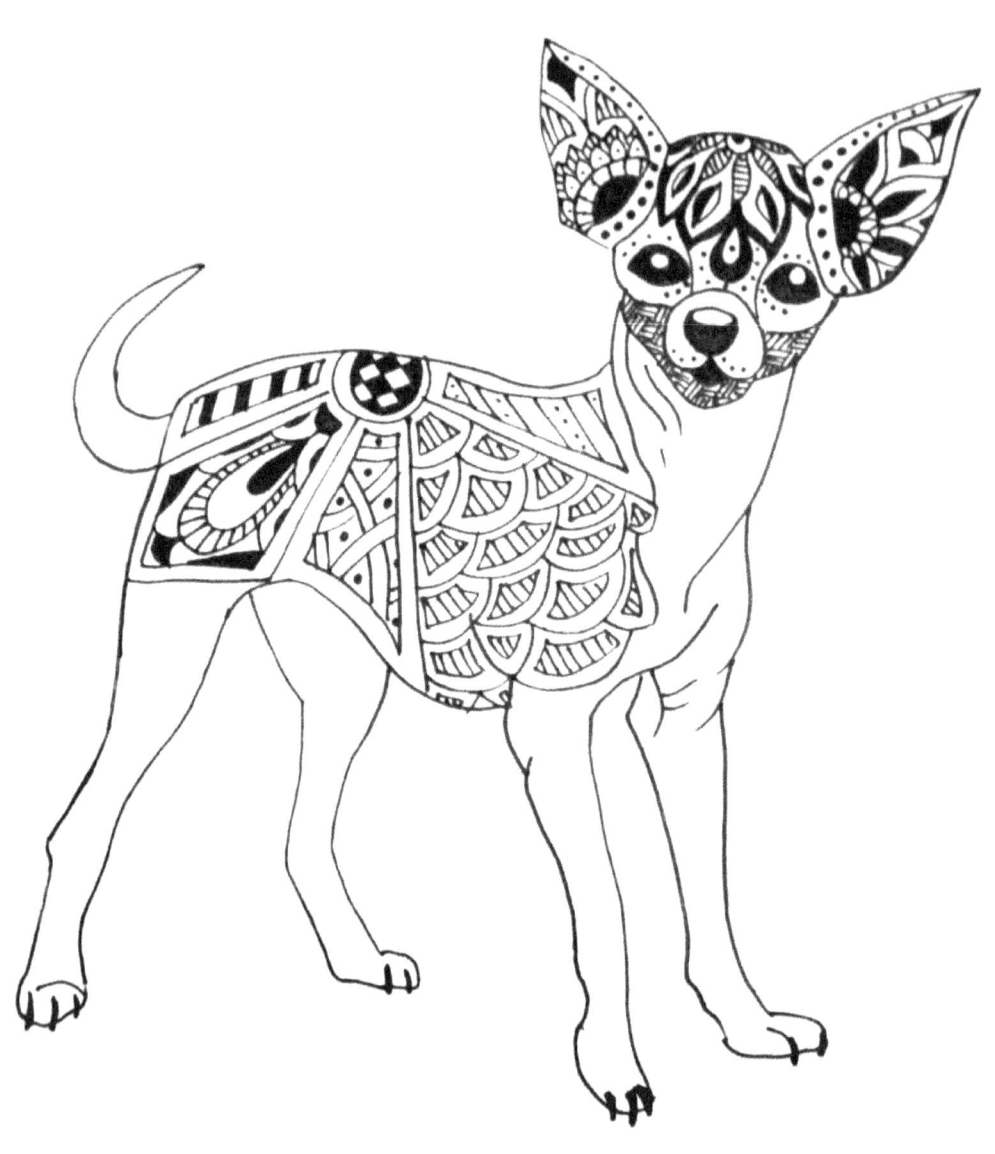

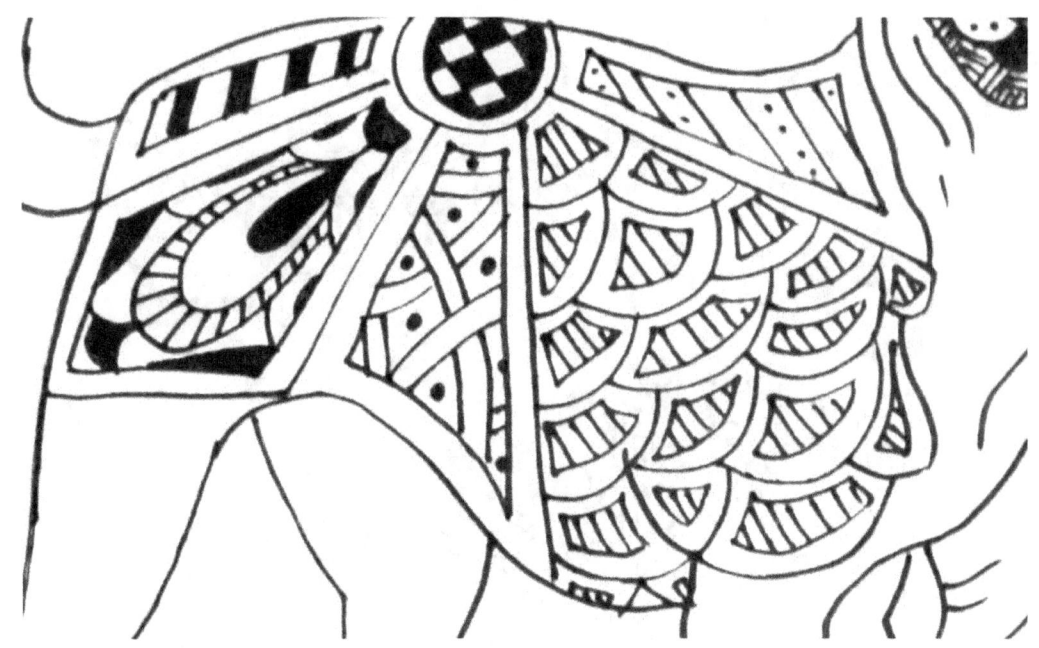

As we have outlined absolutely the whole back of a Chihuahua, we can move on to her small, elongated neck. The neck, as you can see in the drawings consists of only one spot pattern. Nothing difficult, but links the back and the head.

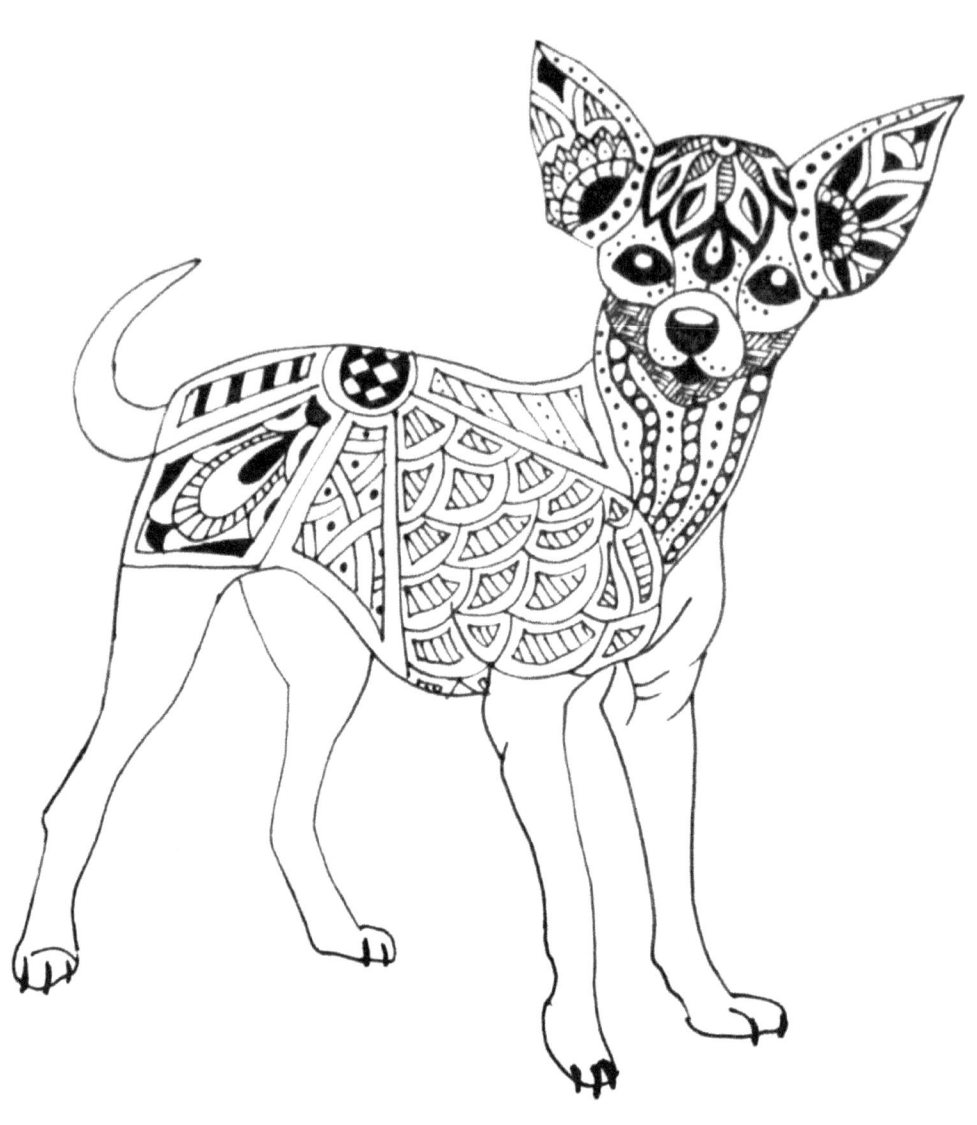

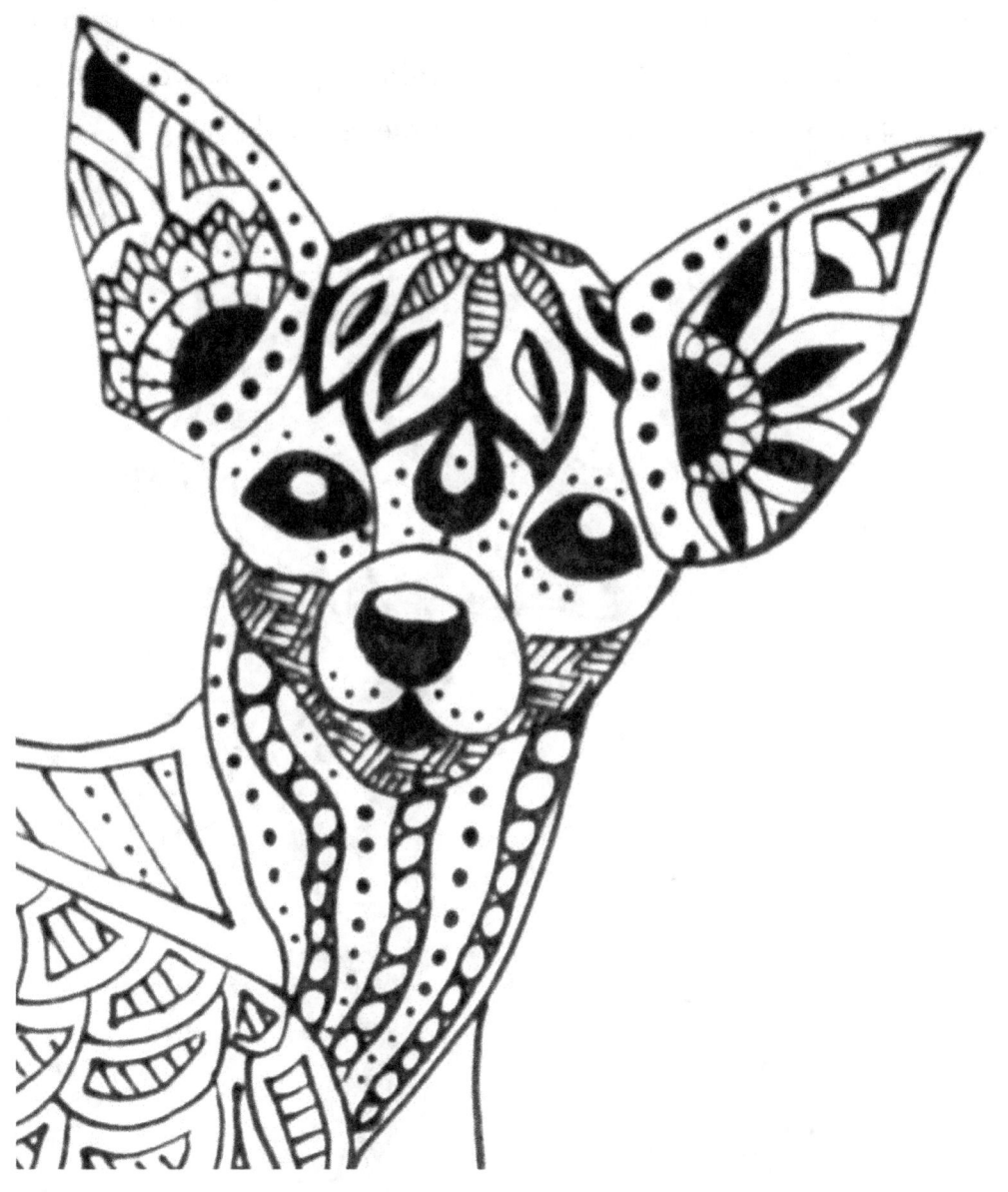

Now, we came to those cute, tiny legs, but filled with various Zen patterns. There are actually three patterns on Chi back legs. The right leg is easier to draw, so pay more attention to the left one. There is a same pattern but split in two and colored differently.

The front leg on the second picture is really something! I recommend that you draw those white laces first with an ordinary pencil so you wouldn`t make a mistake. It is easy afterwards to color the rest of the leg.

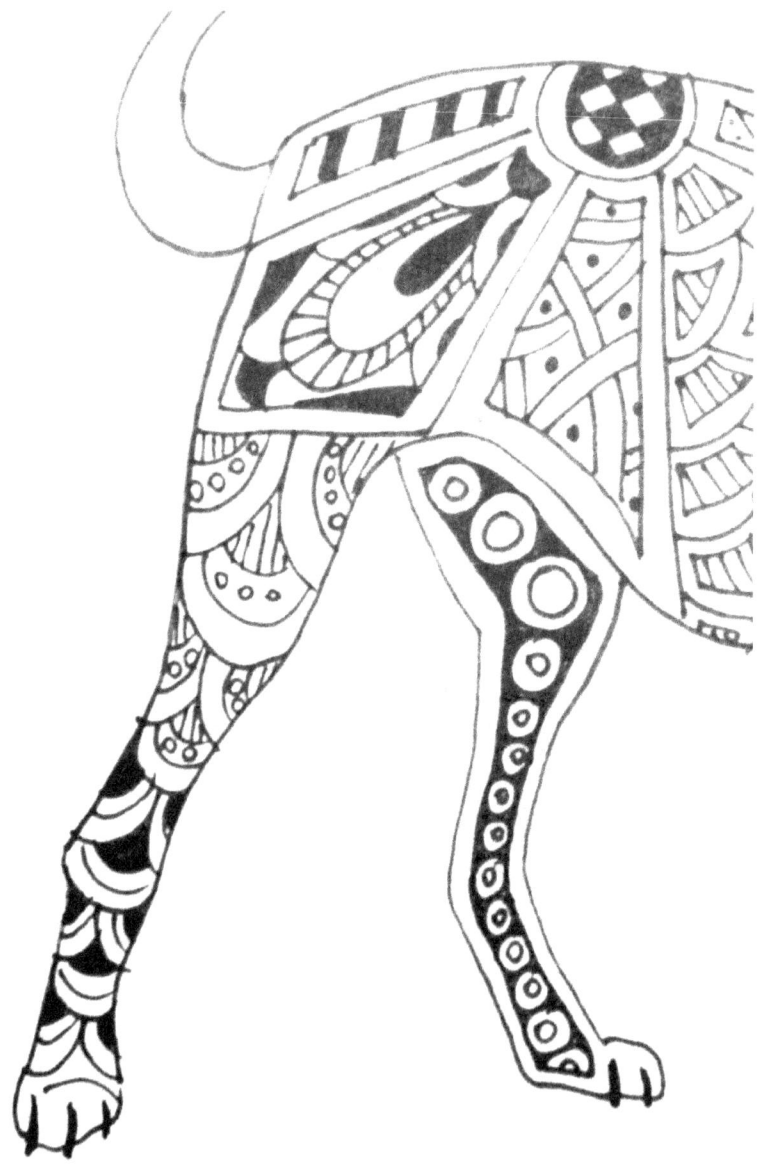

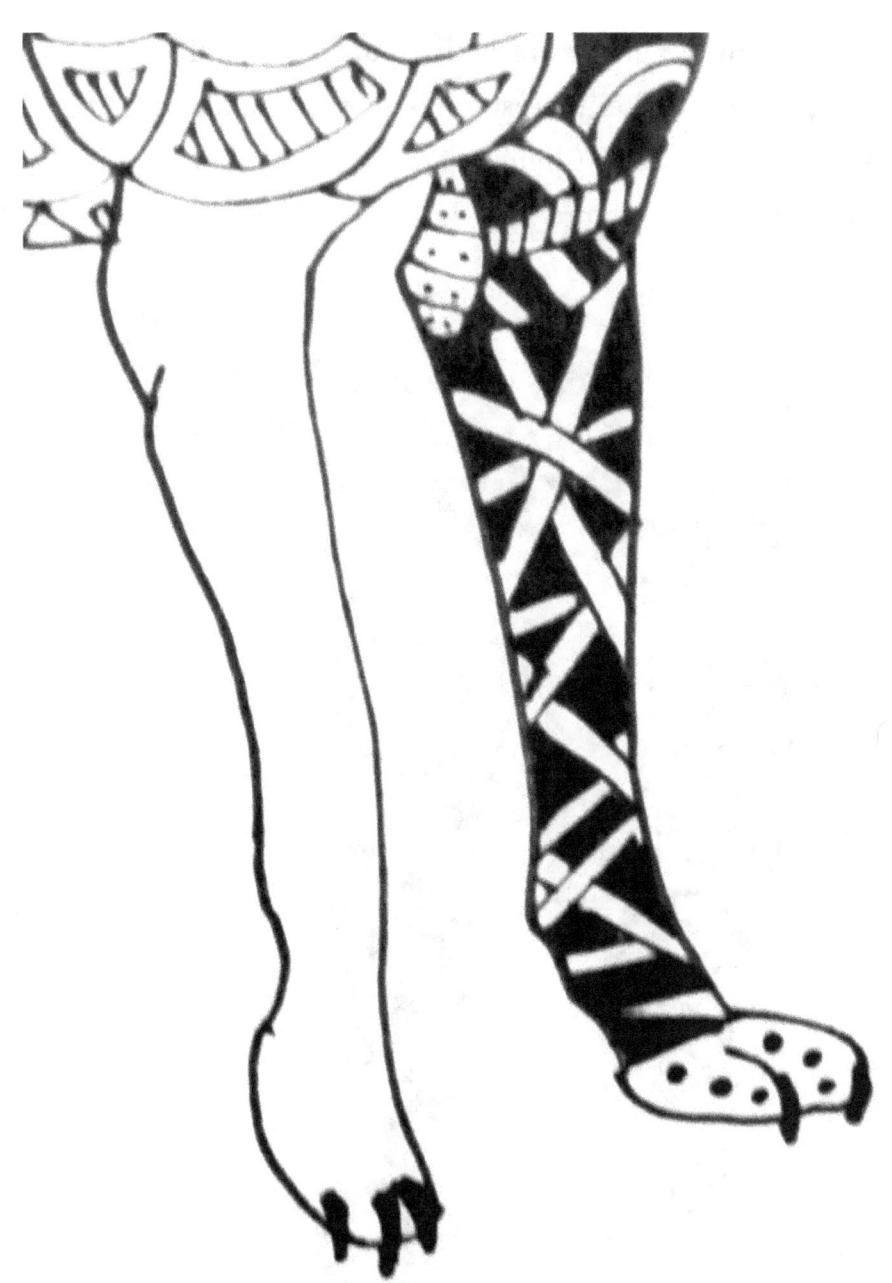

On the last two drawings of our finished Chihuahua, you can see the pattern on its last leg and it`s quite interesting as there are many different forms. The first picture below shows Chihuahua`s forth leg zoomed so you can see it better and the second picture is a finished Zen doodle of this tiny, but angry dog.

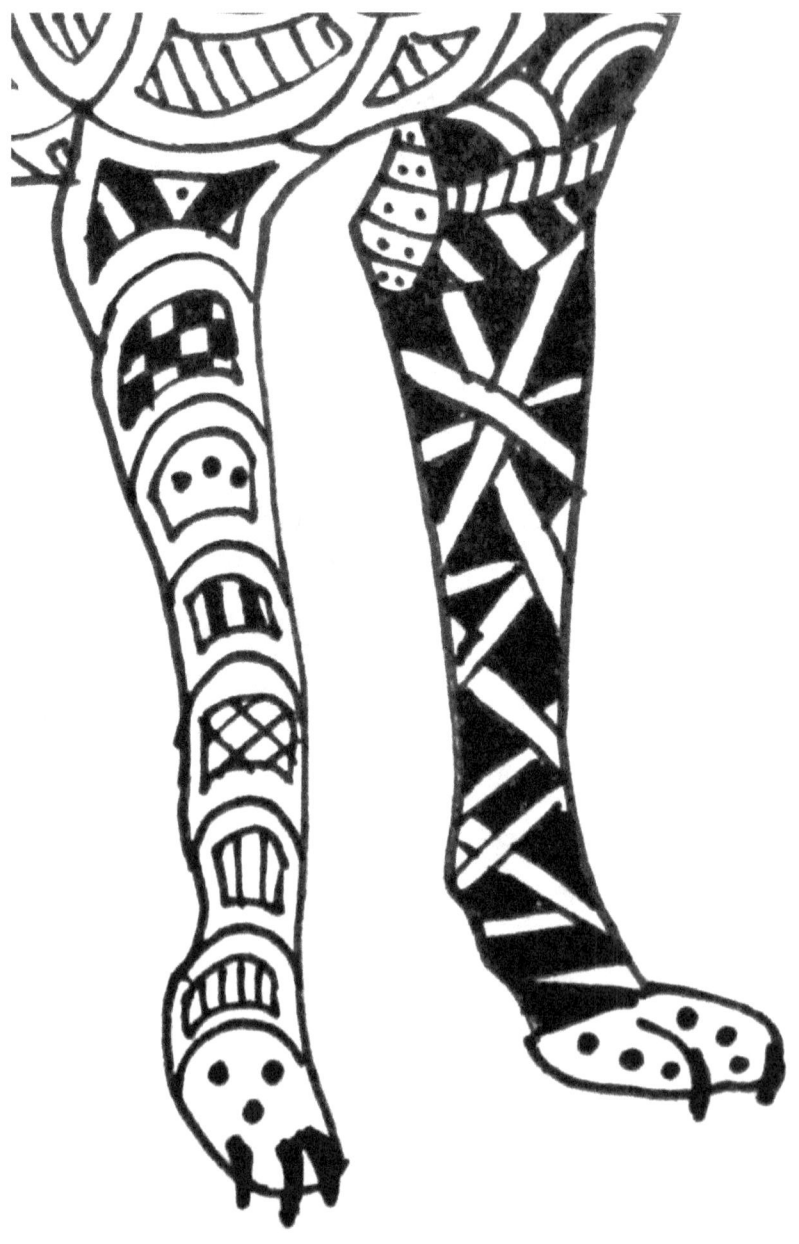

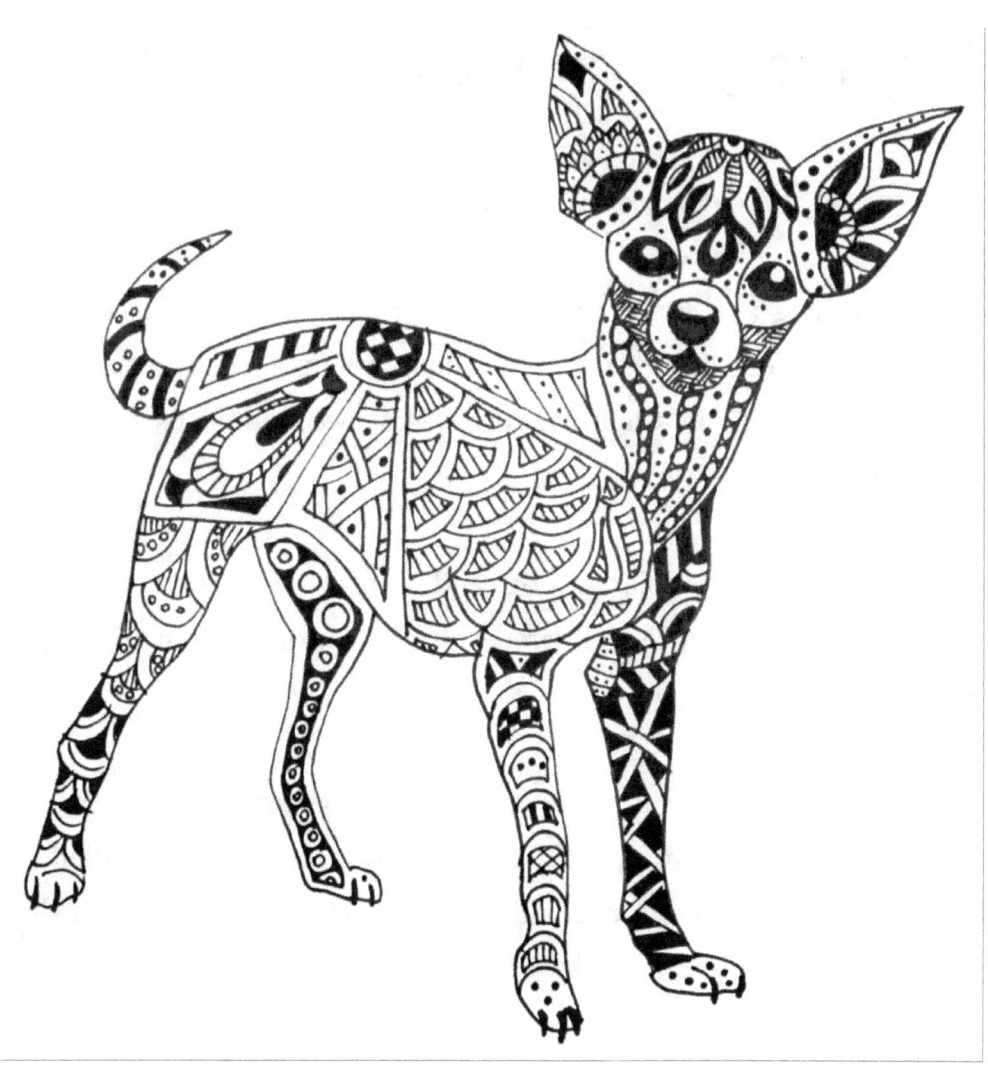

Chapter 3- Zen Beagle: the Head

The idea was that the next Zen doodle dog represents my favorite breed, and it's a beagle. I'll always be sorry that I live in the building and cannot have this beautiful dog as a pet because he is a hunting dog and needs a lot of space to run. If you did not know the most famous beagle in the world is Snoopy from a cartoon Charlie Brown. Now we will focus only on his beautiful head.

Beagle is otherwise very playful dog, and so it shows on the drawing, his keeps his mouth open since he is tired of running around all the time. Don`t you just love a beagle?

The first drawing below is a pretty large one so you could catch all the lines that make an expression on his face, so I advise you to be very patient with this one. Look at his jaw, a tongue and lines that surround his eyes. It should all be a bit bolded so you won`t lose those lines afterwards.

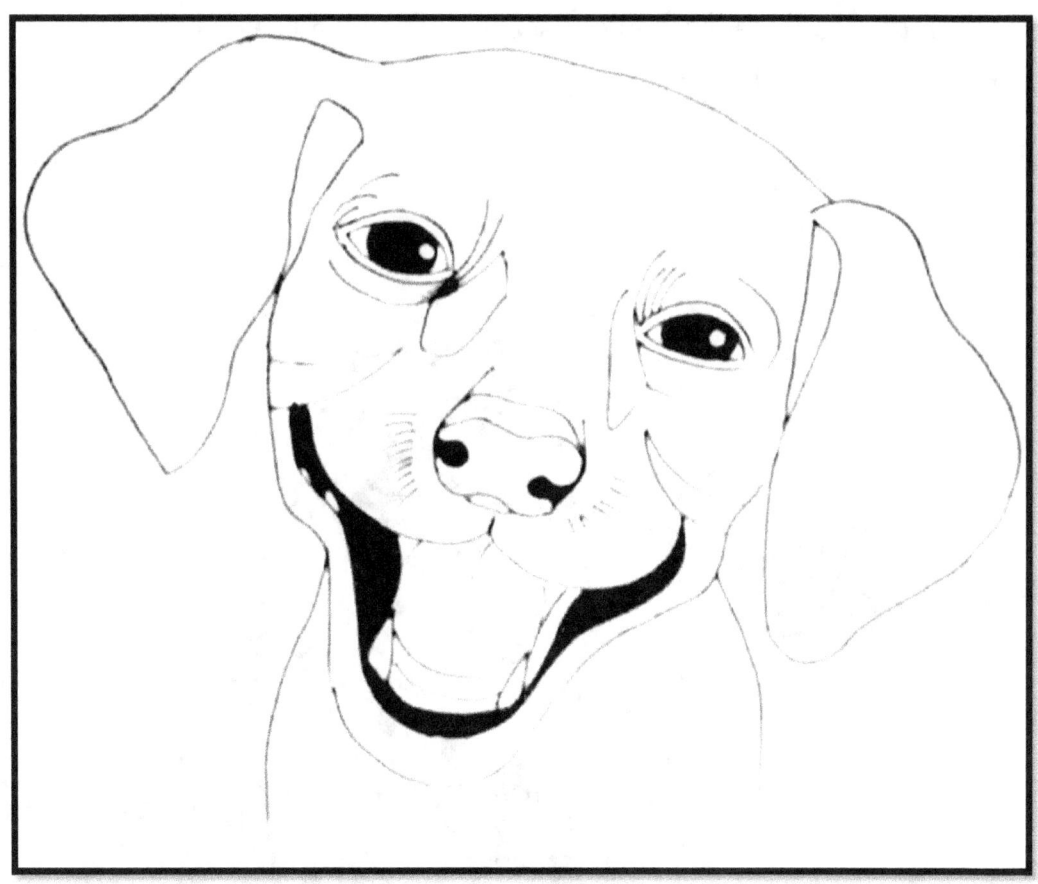

Next, we will move on to his ears as they are also very significant like in Chihuahua`s. Beagle`s ears will be zoomed on the drawings below so you can easily copy the Zen patterns. I forget to mention but you can always change the patterns if you think something would fit better or you like some other Zen doodles more as these are just suggestions and we are just playing in expressing our creativity. So play a bit if you wish!

The first picture shows his right ear, it`s the left side from our perspective, and the second one shows his left ear and, of course, it is right from our point of view. Now, enjoy in filling in beagle`s cute ears.

On the third picture below, you can see how your Zen beagle could look like after he gets his Zen doodle ears.

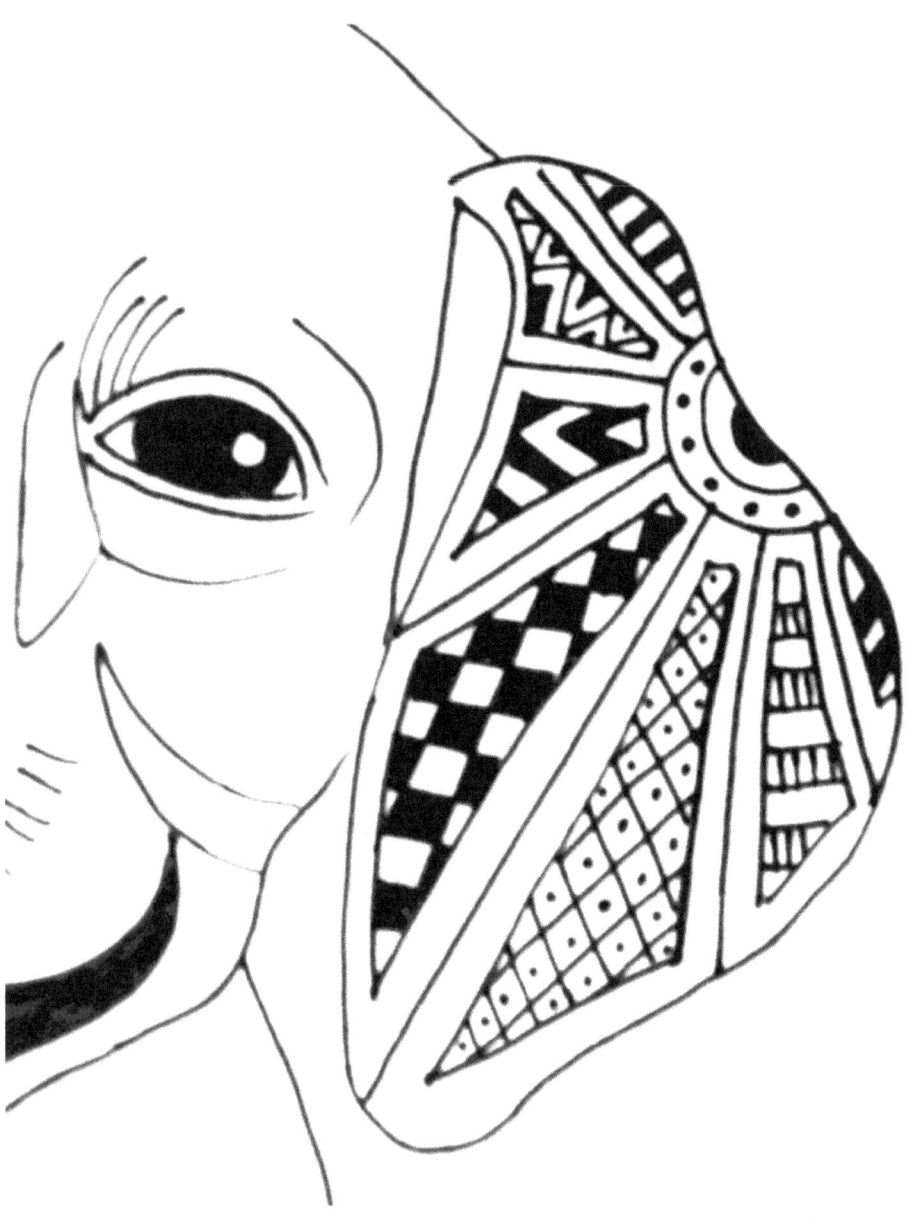

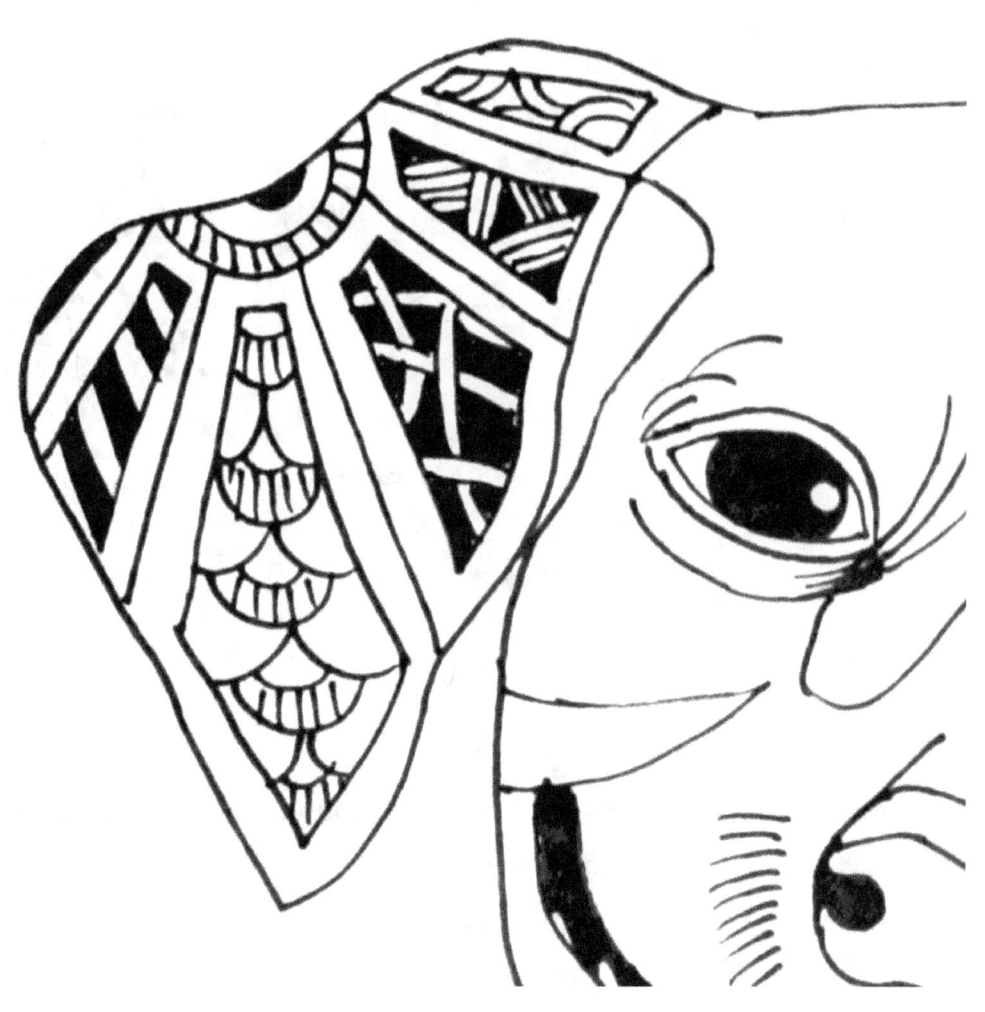

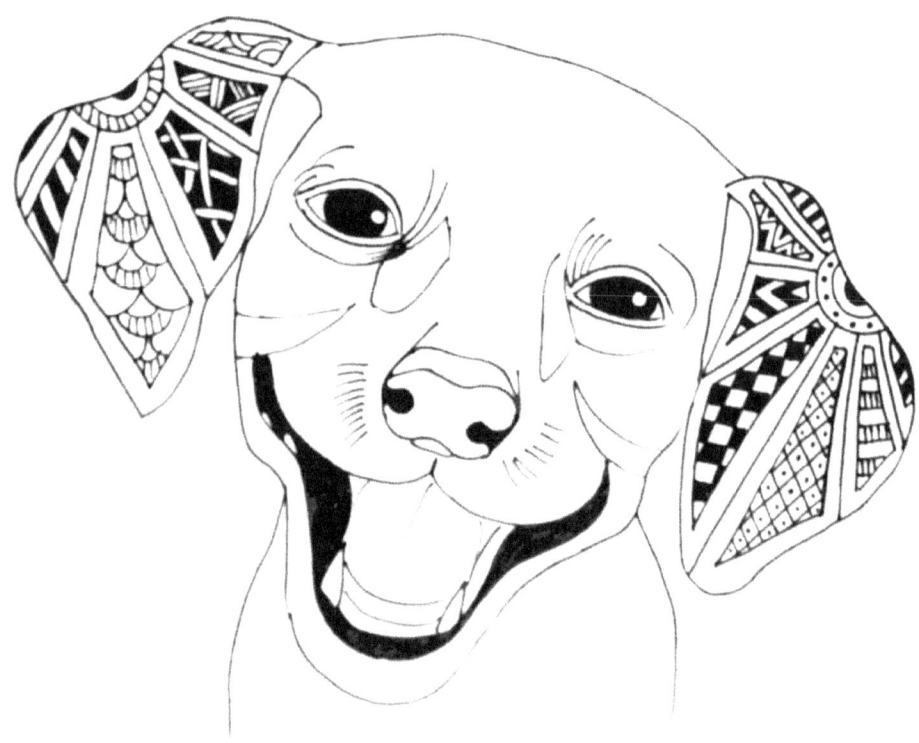

Let us now fill the part of his jaw and parts around. Those are rather simple patterns cause you cannot make everything tangled because of the contrast and cause you wouldn`t see anything. Below is a picture of beagle`s head without his ears so you could focus on that.

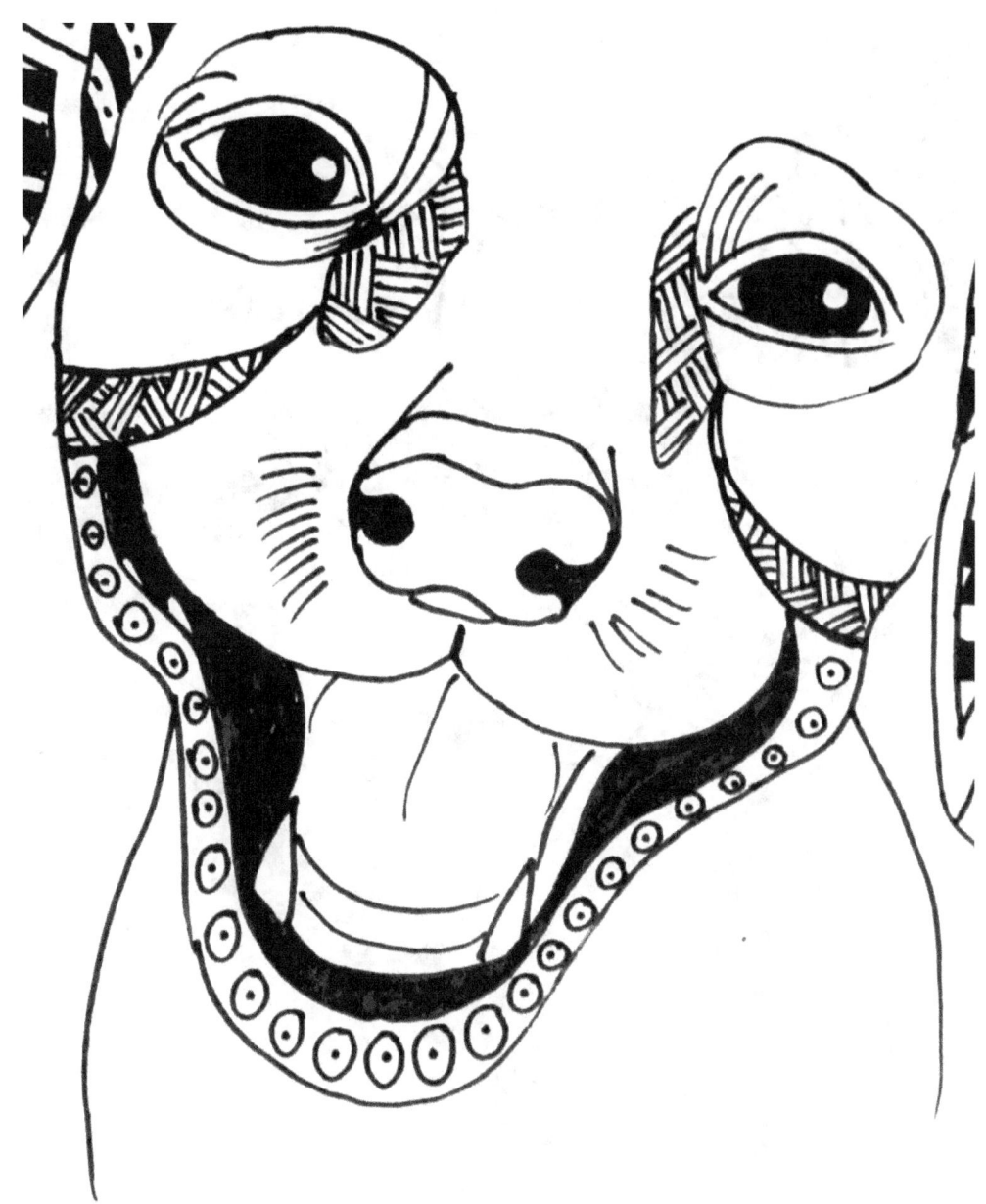

We can now embellish his eyes by drawing something that looks like a royal jewelry on his head and around his eyes. On the first picture below you will find his decorated face and on the second one how he should look like after all the mentioned and shown Zen patterns are drawn.

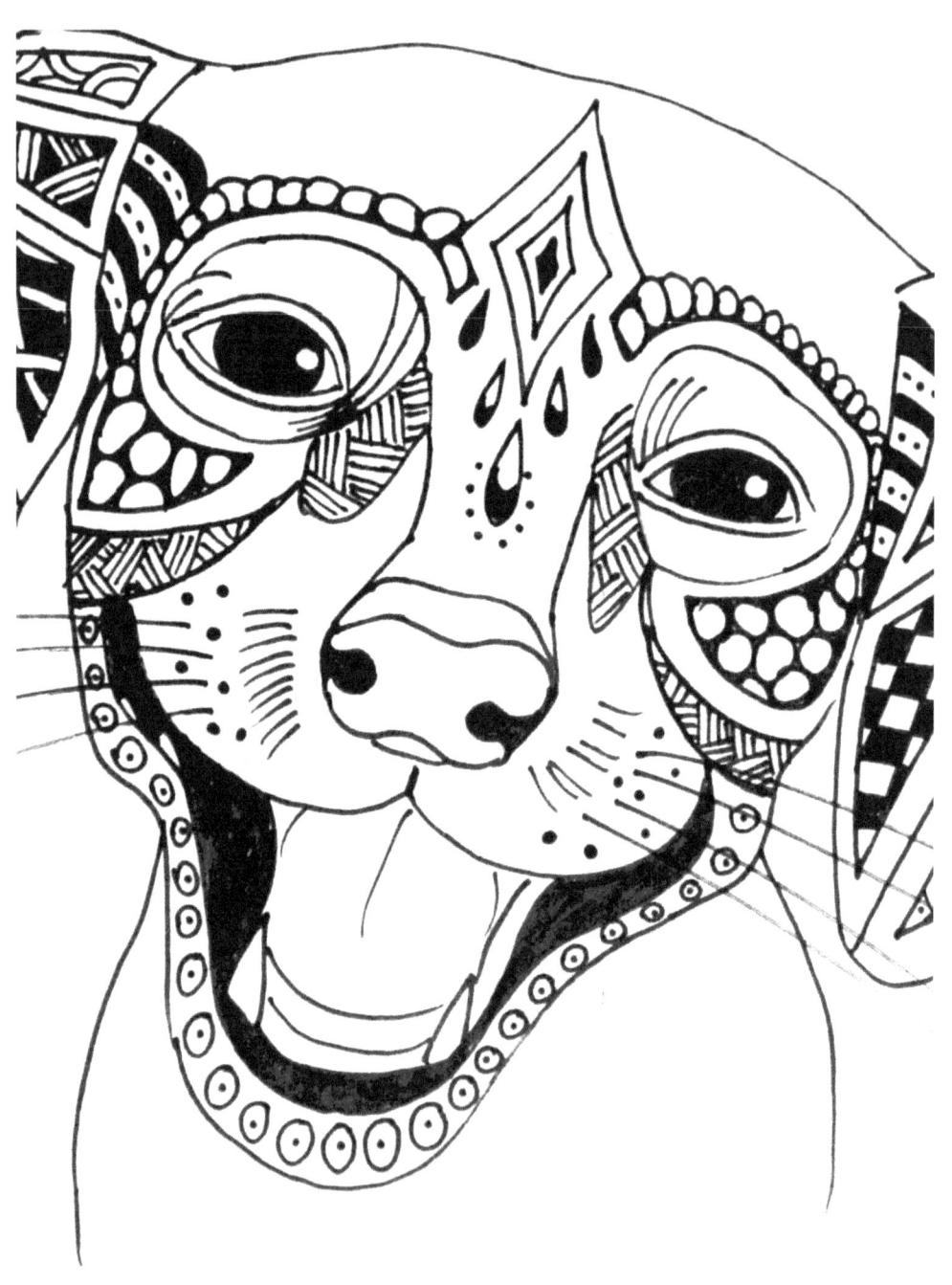

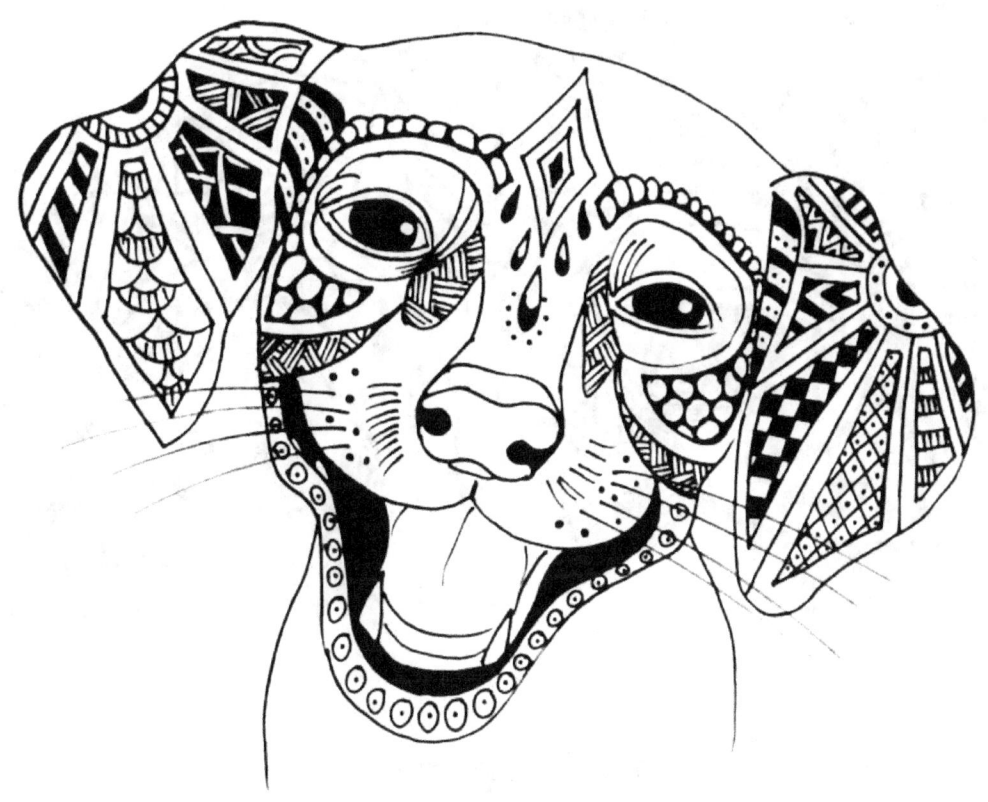

, we will decorate his forehead with a similar pattern we used for his ears, it looks like some rhombs and rhomboids as you can see on the picture below, it seems like royalty, doesn`t it? His forehead is shown a bit closer on the second drawing below.

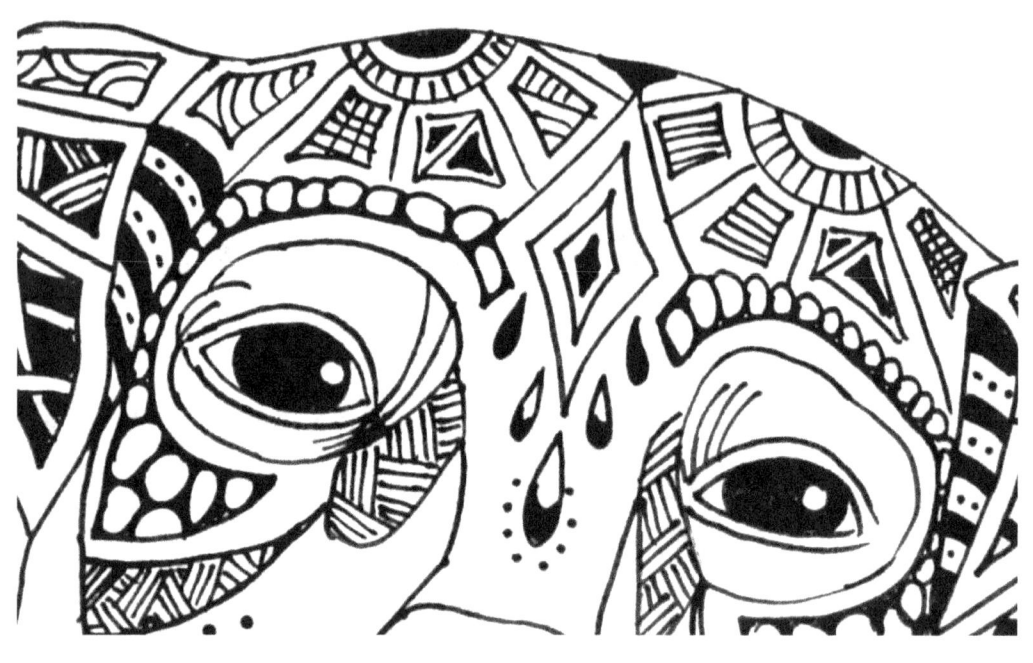

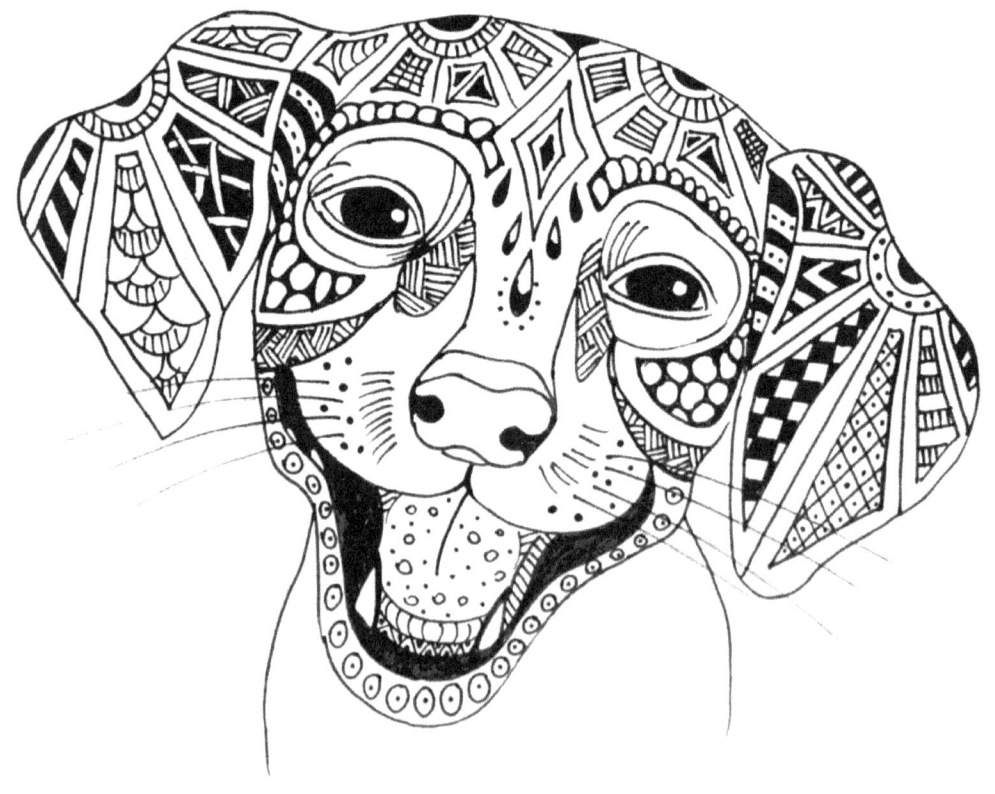

We came to the end of drawing our happy Zen doodle beagle and we just have to make his neck a bit interesting as shown on the drawings below. The first drawing shows his neck in detail while the second one displays the finished Zen drawing of a beagle. Do not forget his dotty tongue, it contributes to his playfulness.

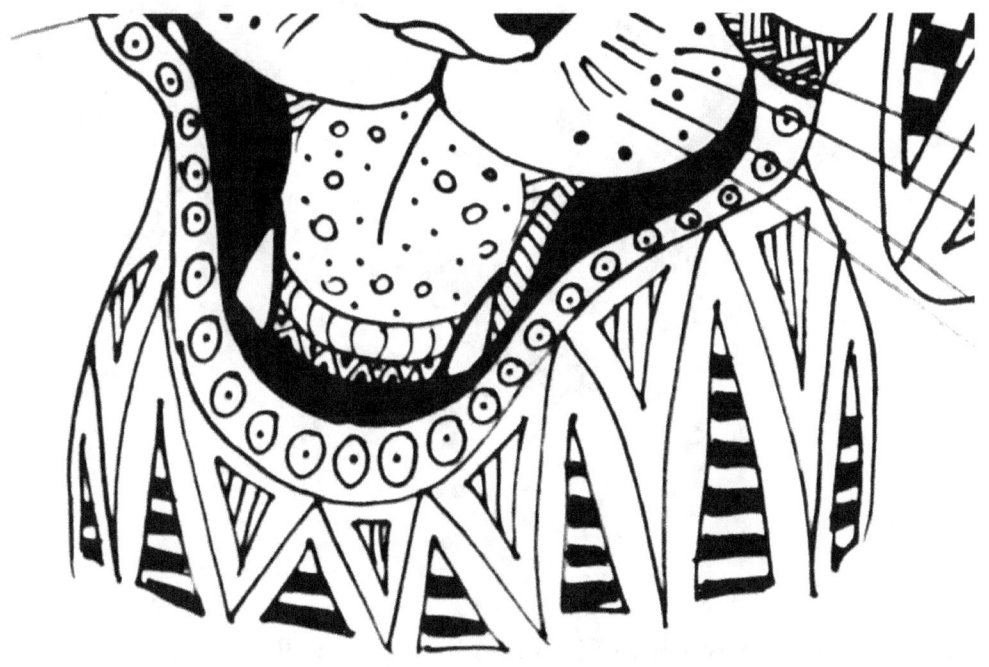

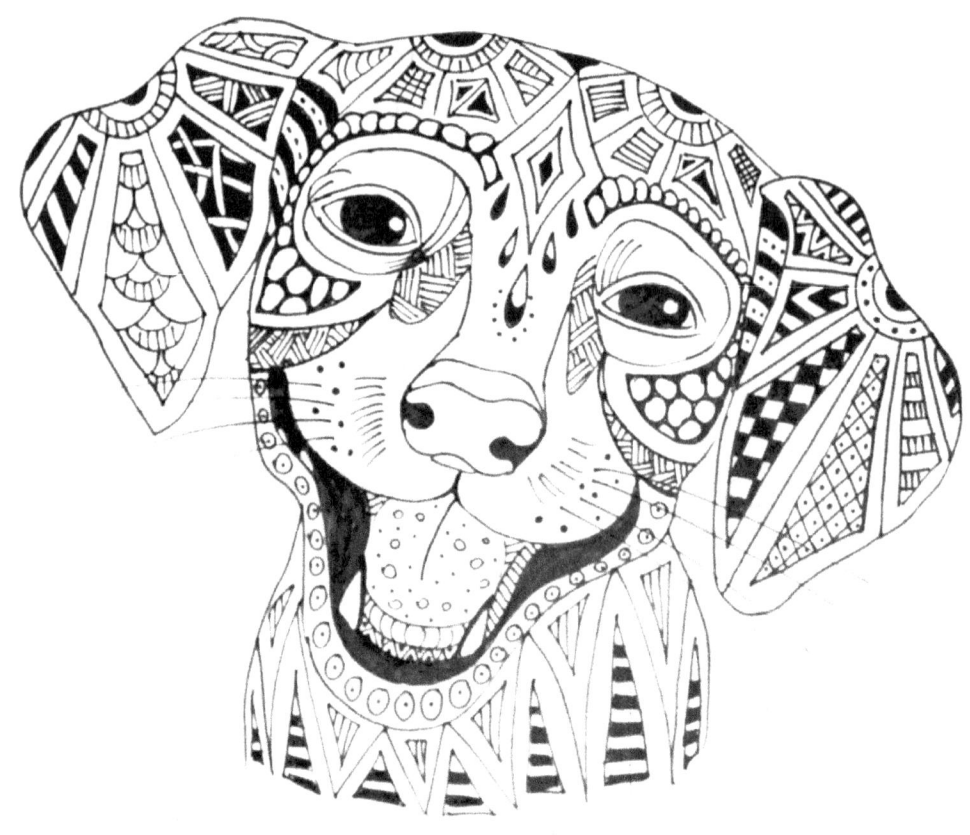

Guess who is next on our list of Zen doodle dogs? Well, it`s a...

Chapter 4- Zen Basset

Although the great hunter of rabbits, today basset is commonly kept as a pet and a show dog. This breed is basically playful, friendly, agile and active. By nature they are very tolerant and therefore are excellent pets for families with children or other animals. Bassets are intelligent and very easily trained with the right motivation, which in their case is food. They love to eat and will quickly understand what is required of them in order to get a treat. People wrongly believe that the Basset is stubborn which is not true. They are just very sensitive and closed if you use punishment as a training method. So, do not punish your basset hound, but give him to eat!

The figure below shows the basic shape of the basset`s body that is very wrinkled and therefore the drawing is a bit large for you to be able to see all the frills on his skin and transfer them easily to your drawing

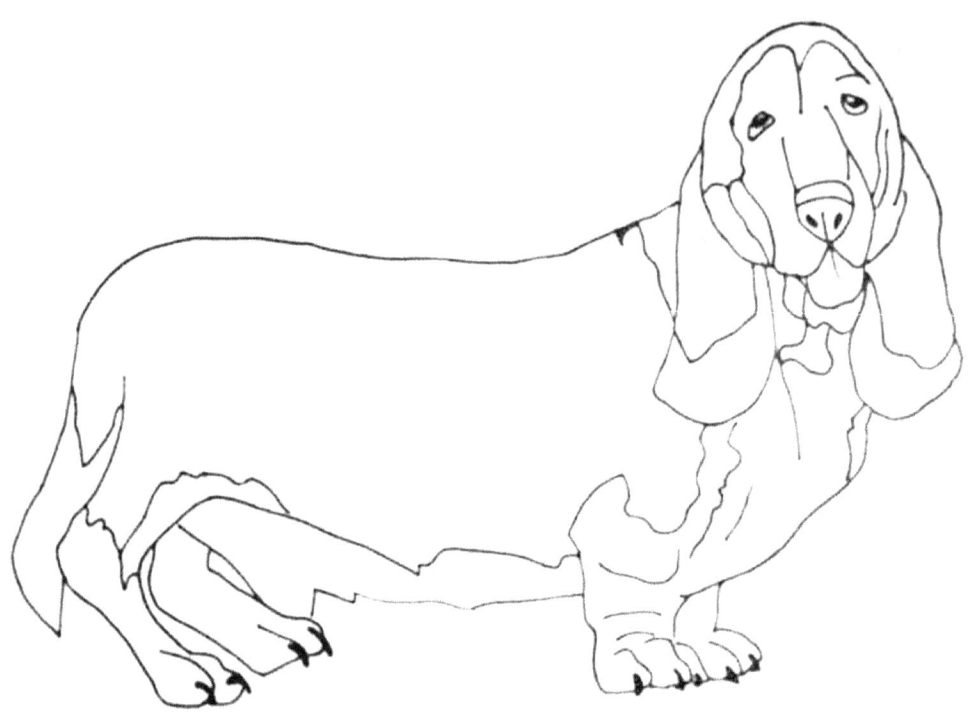

Now, in the middle of his back that resembles a playground we will draw a circle with gentle patterns inside as shown on the drawings below. The first one is what I called "a gentle pattern "in a circle and the second pictures shows the whole basset so you could know where on his back to draw it.

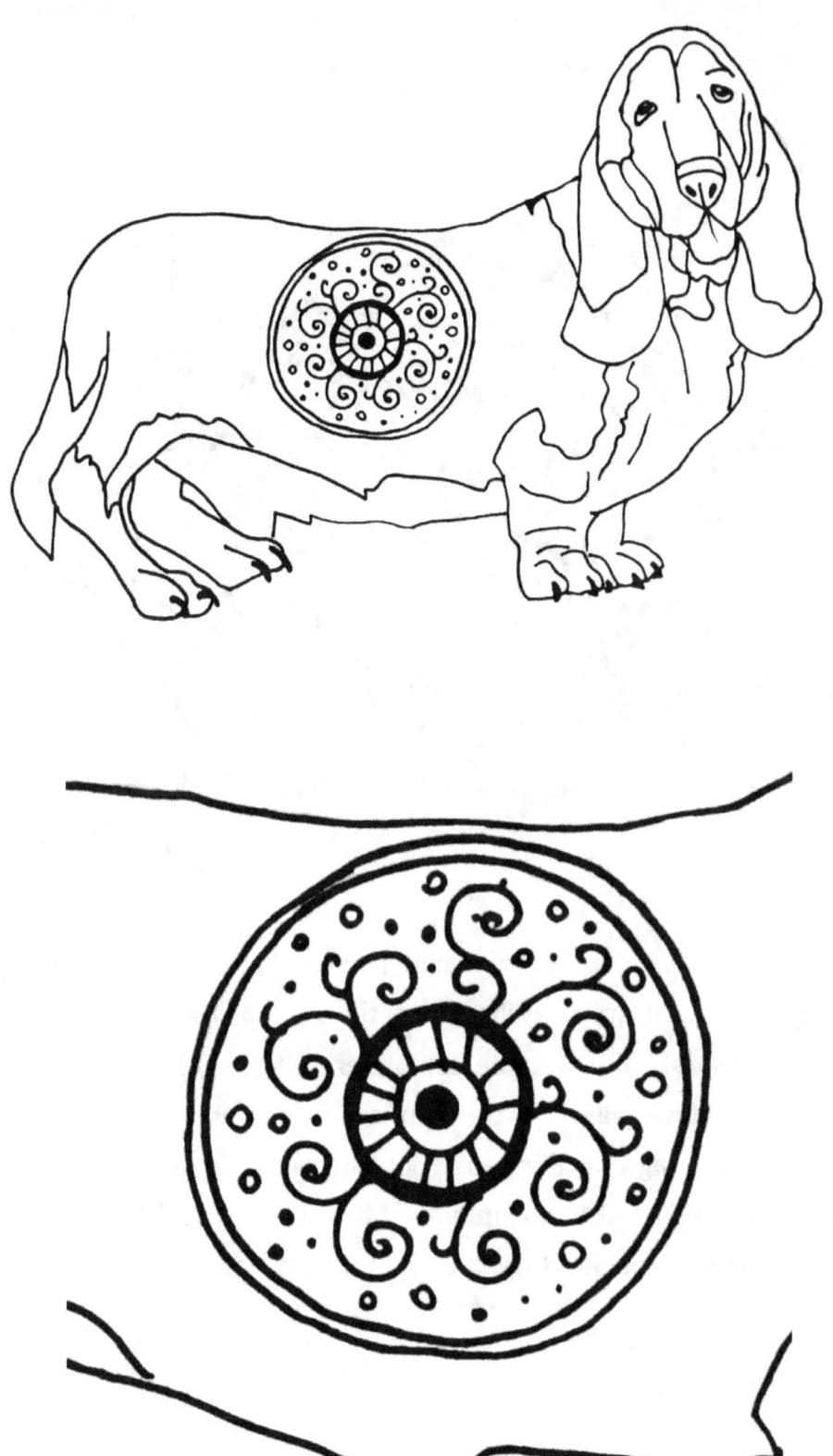

We will now embellish the circle on basset`s back with interesting petals as displayed on the drawing on the right. It`s not that hard, is it?

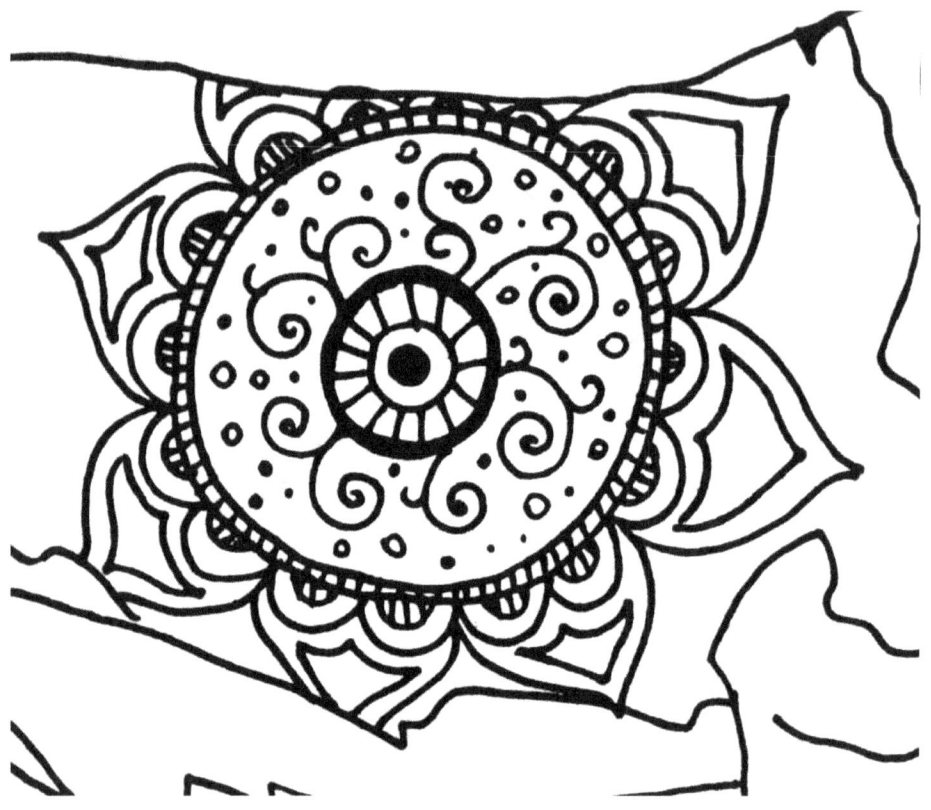

Now let's expand the decorative forms on the whole basset`s back. It may look like a beautiful quilt as shown on the first picture below. The first picture includes only the awesome Zen pattern on dog`s back. Take a closer look to see in which way I have expanded the pattern since there aren`t strict limits, meaning that the pattern on the following drawings is spread on basset`s leg and a tail till the middle of it. On the second picture, you can see how he should look after this step.

The drawings are deliberately enlarged for you to be able to recognize the complexity of the lines and shapes as the body of a basset hound, as I already said, is extremely wrinkled, and asymmetrical. Your focus must be undivided if you wish to draw the doodles right, but then again, that is the point of Zen-ability to keep your attention steady.

Just look at him. It`s a cute fat dog with short legs and a sad look on his face.

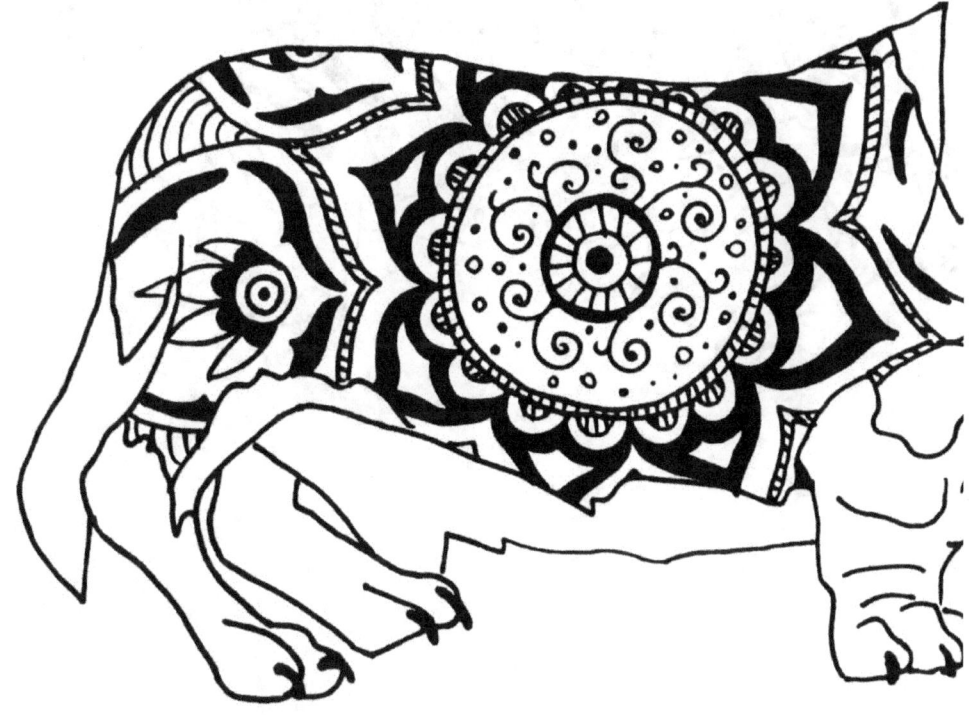

You must be wondering what is the next part of basset`s body we will be filling out with Zen doodles! As you can see in the picture below, we will draw doodles on the lower part of his ears, the rest of the tail, as well as the lower part of the body, which, by the way, looks like a Swiss cheese. The drawing is greatly increased, so you will have no problem to see what and where to draw, just as always when we do the Zen tangled patterns-slowly and carefully!

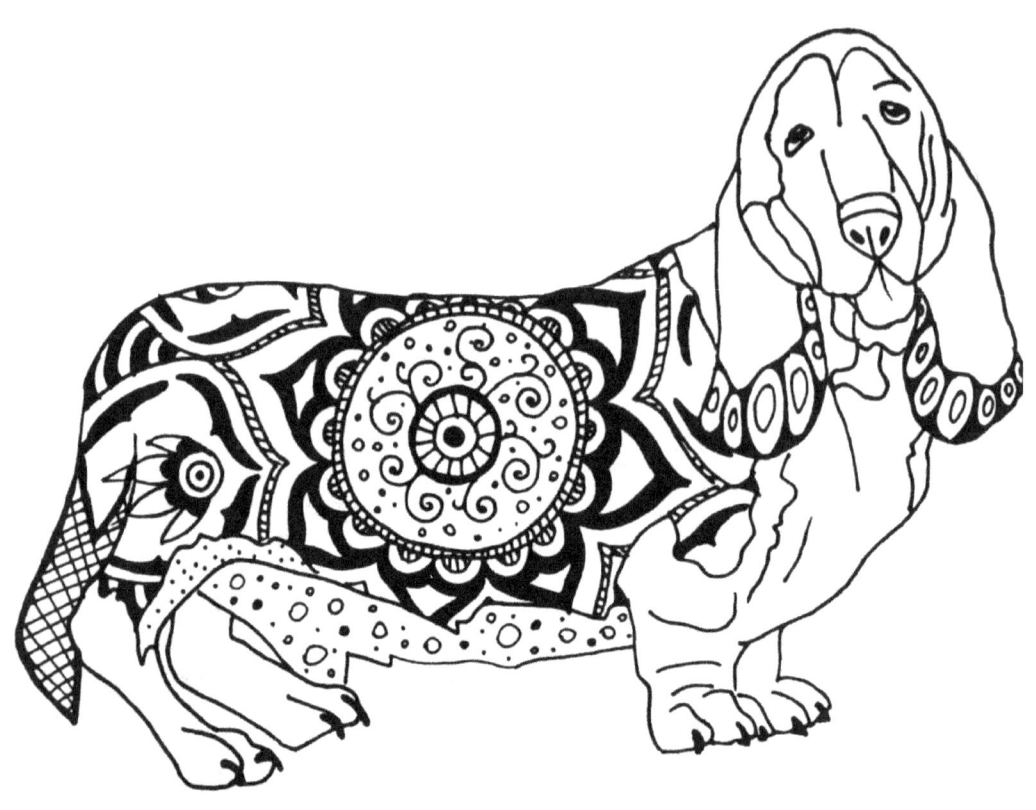

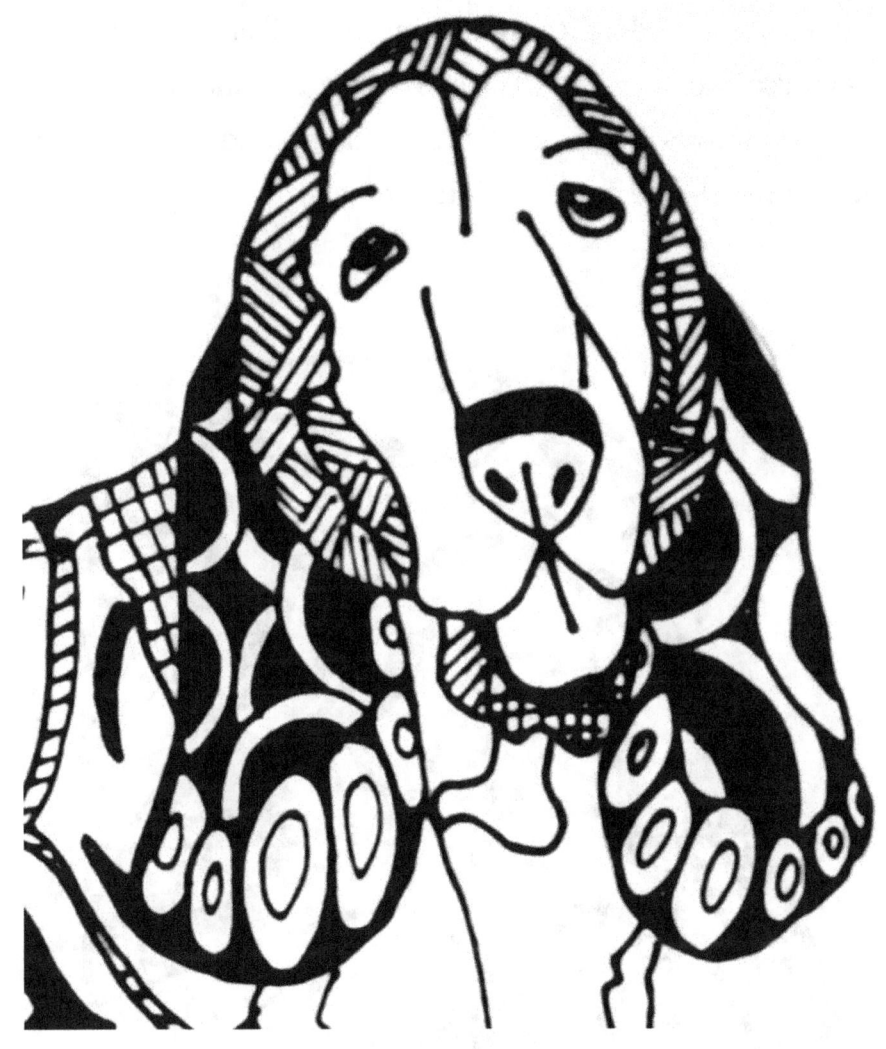

The following will be his long ears and an outer part of his face as you can see on a zoomed drawing on the left. Do not forget this thick black line across his snout.

Do not be cheated by these seemingly simple patterns on basset`s ears and the outer part of the face. They are not plain at all and require full concentration and reflection. Doesn`t he look sad? He reminds me of a left boyfriend.

So, what is our next step? Our next steps will include embellishing his crumpled chest with Zen doodles and fixing his tail a bit to look more noticeable. Just use your black marker and follow the lines on a tail. First drawing below shows his improved tail and the second one displays his wrinkled chest so you should pay more attention to it.

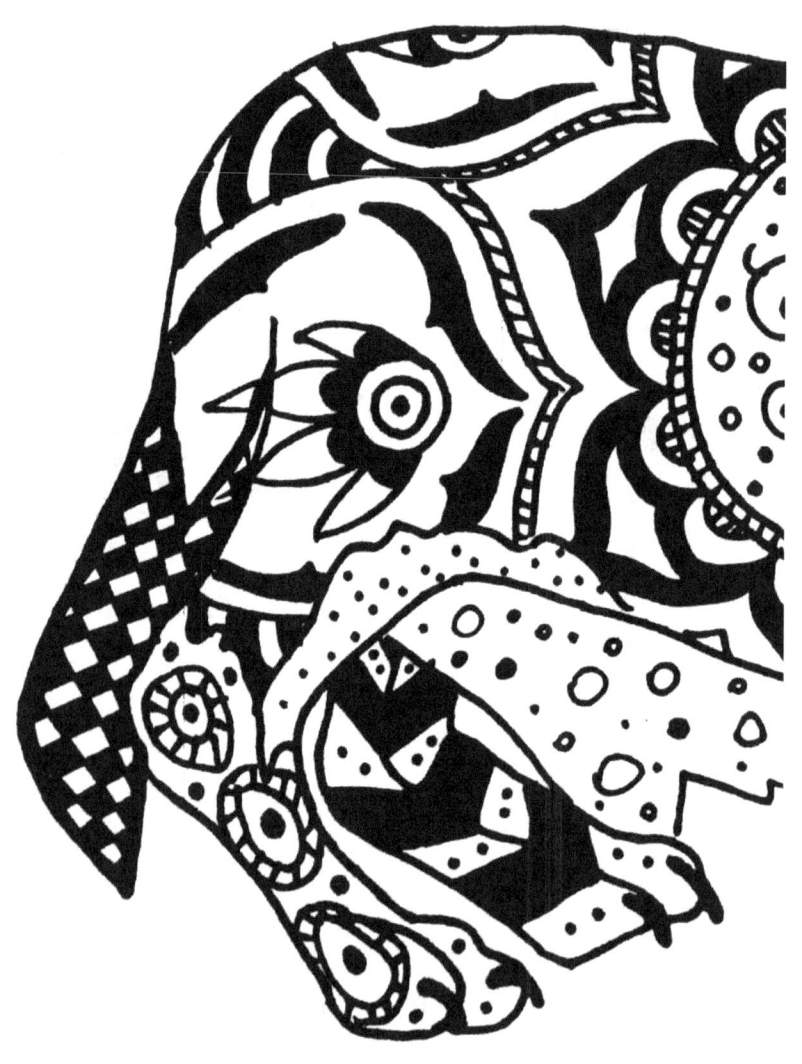

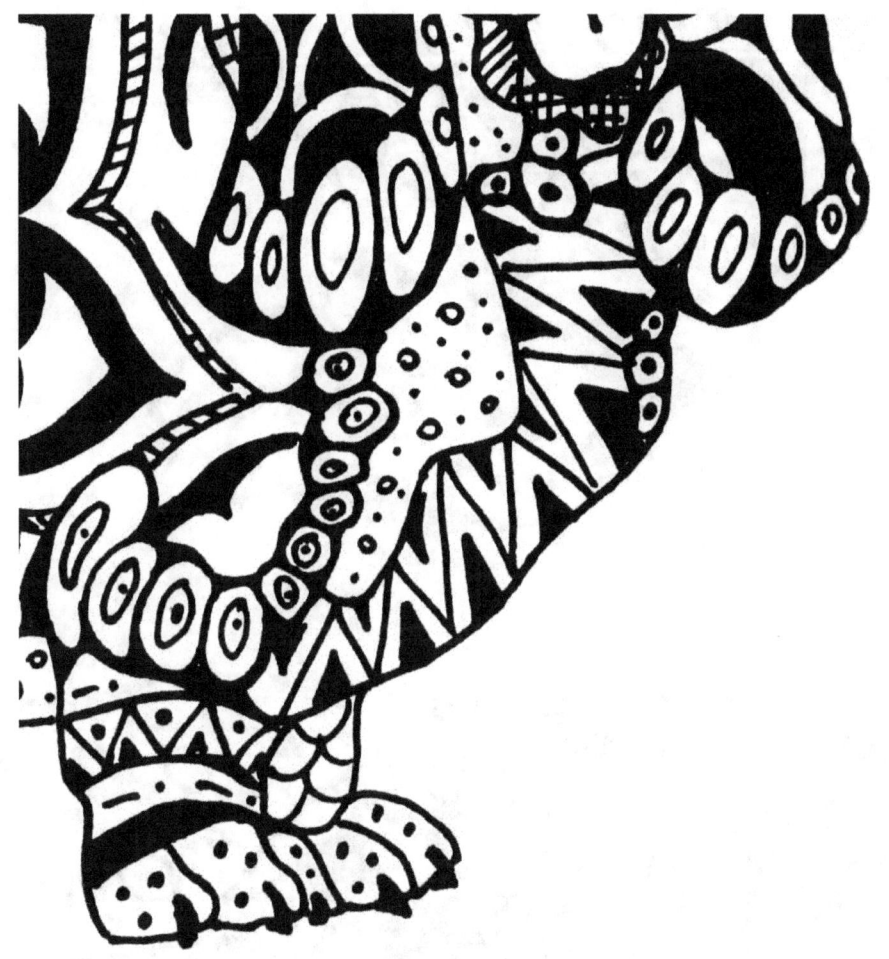

Finally, what we have left to complete our sad looking basset? I believe it`s his legs and a face. So, let`s take a look at explanatory drawings below to see how to make our Zen basset whole by filling out his short legs since we are going to leave his face as it is because of the contrast and we don`t want to lose that specific expression on his face. His cute little front legs are shown on the first picture below, and on the second one, you can take a closer look on his back legs.

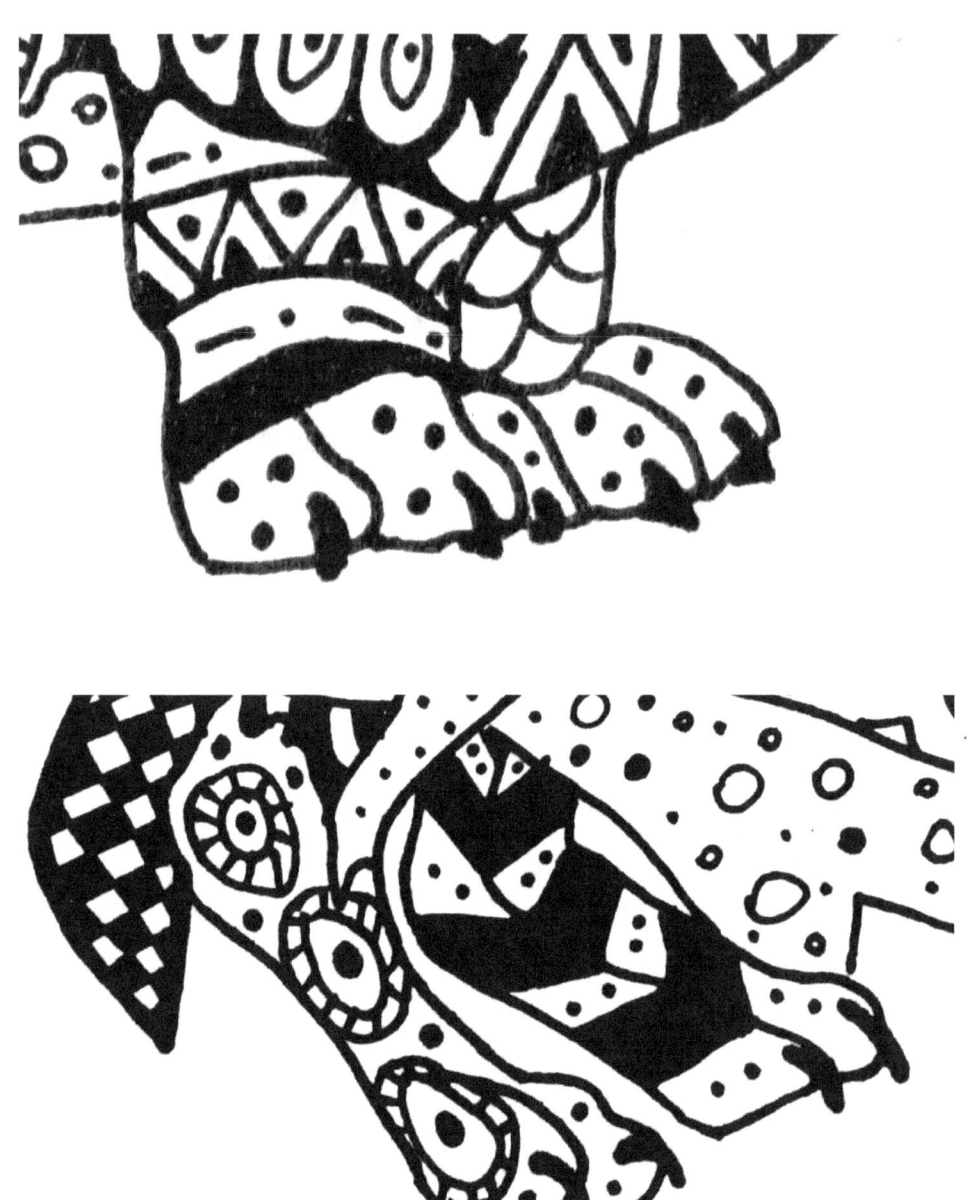

Below you can see the whole drawing in case you missed something or something isn`t quite clear to you.

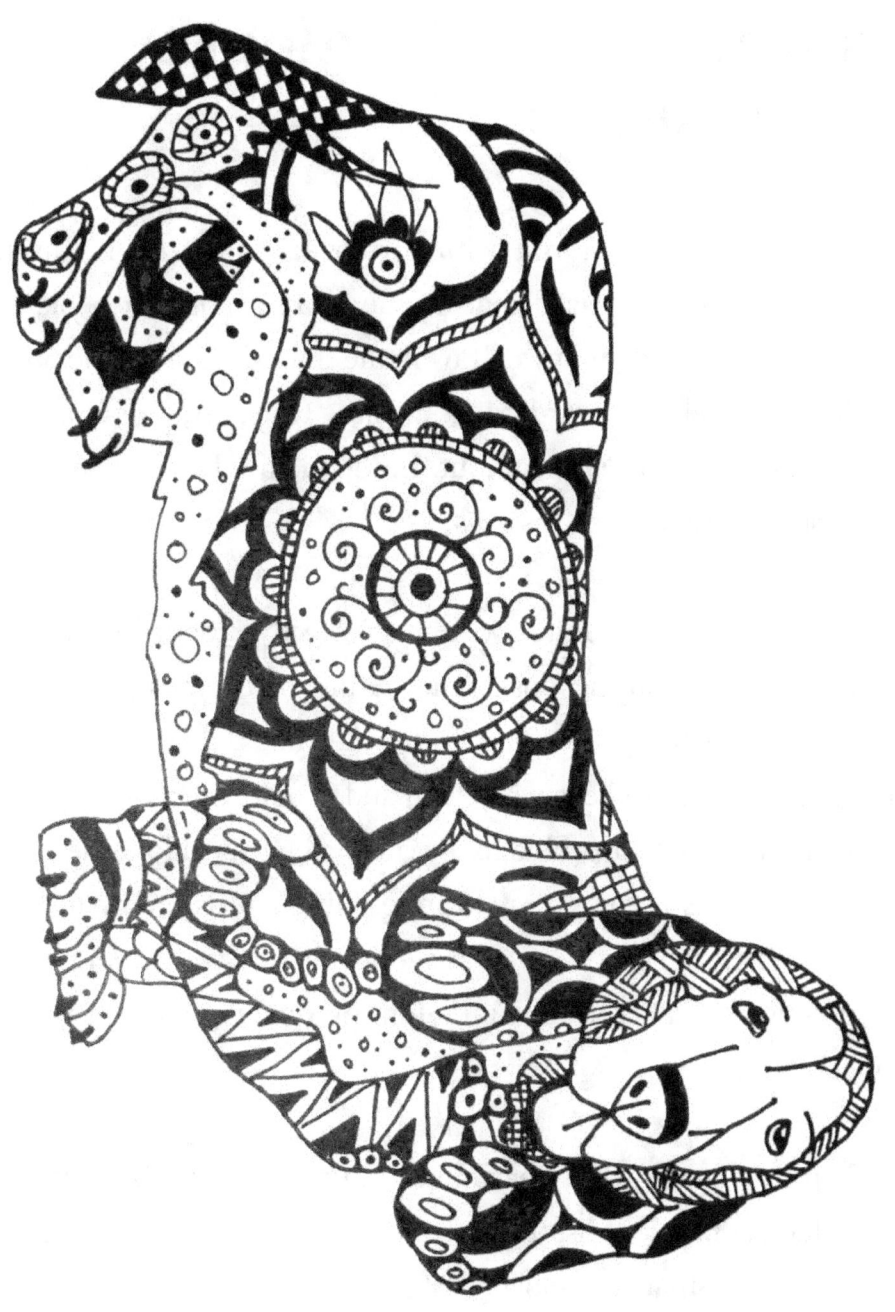

Now, we will draw another beagle, but the whole figure. You will be able to see his raised tail while he waits for the right moment to go on a hunt.

Chapter 5- Zen Beagle: the Whole Figure

I have already introduced you with my love and affection towards the beagle, so do not be surprised that he shows up again in a book, but in a different way. The beagle that we draw in the third chapter of the book was a happy dog that looks forward to its owner. However, the beagle in this drawing is on alert and ready to hunt. In the picture below, you can see his recognizable mottle between his eyes.

Let's get a little more acquainted with this perfectly proportioned dog before we draw him in a hunting pose! The nature of the beagle is sweet and friendly both with the people and with other dogs. Beagles socialize with other dogs and the more he is with them and people, the more he is happier. This sometimes leads to problems because when left alone he constantly barks. This breed is naturally gifted in learning and is happy to learn, but there is no sense training him for a service dog as you should not expect unquestioning obedience from him. Hunting qualities of a beagle are not questionable.

If you doubt the beauty of a beagle, keep in mind that this year (2015), in March, a female beagle 'Miss P' won the 139th edition of the Westminster Kennel Club Dog Show, the most prestigious dog show in the United States held in Madison Square Garden in New York City . Miss P (What a cute name for the cute little dog!) won in competition with 2,700 dogs and almost 200 different breeds.

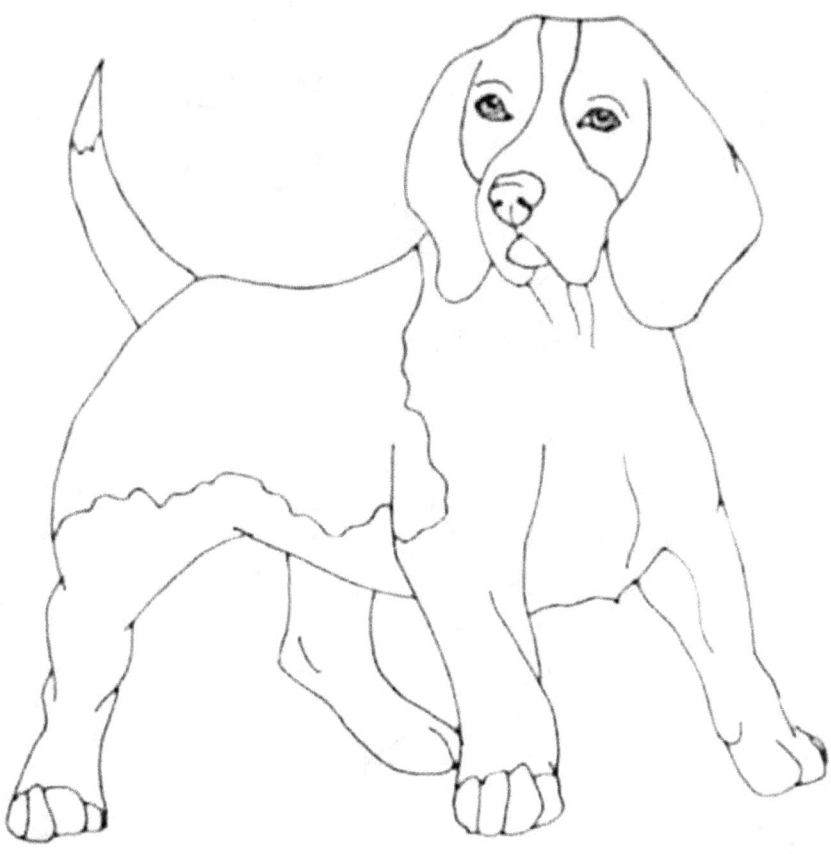

After we draw a basic shape of a beagle, we will add him a flower shape on his back as shown on the pictures below.

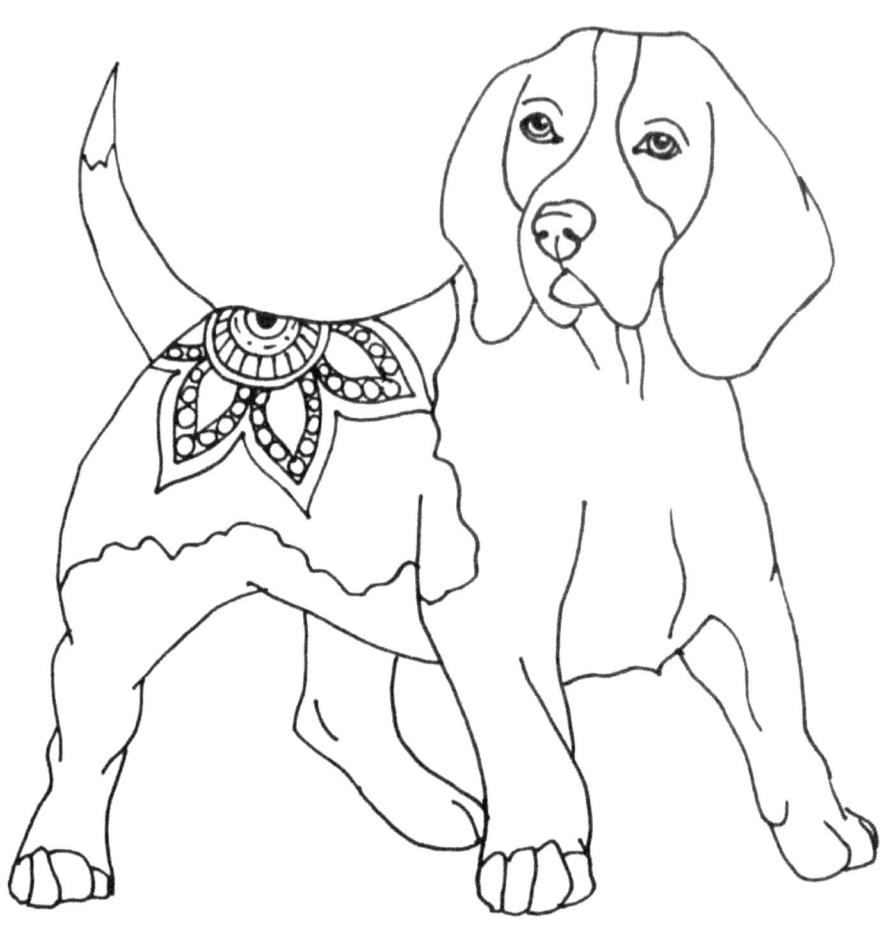

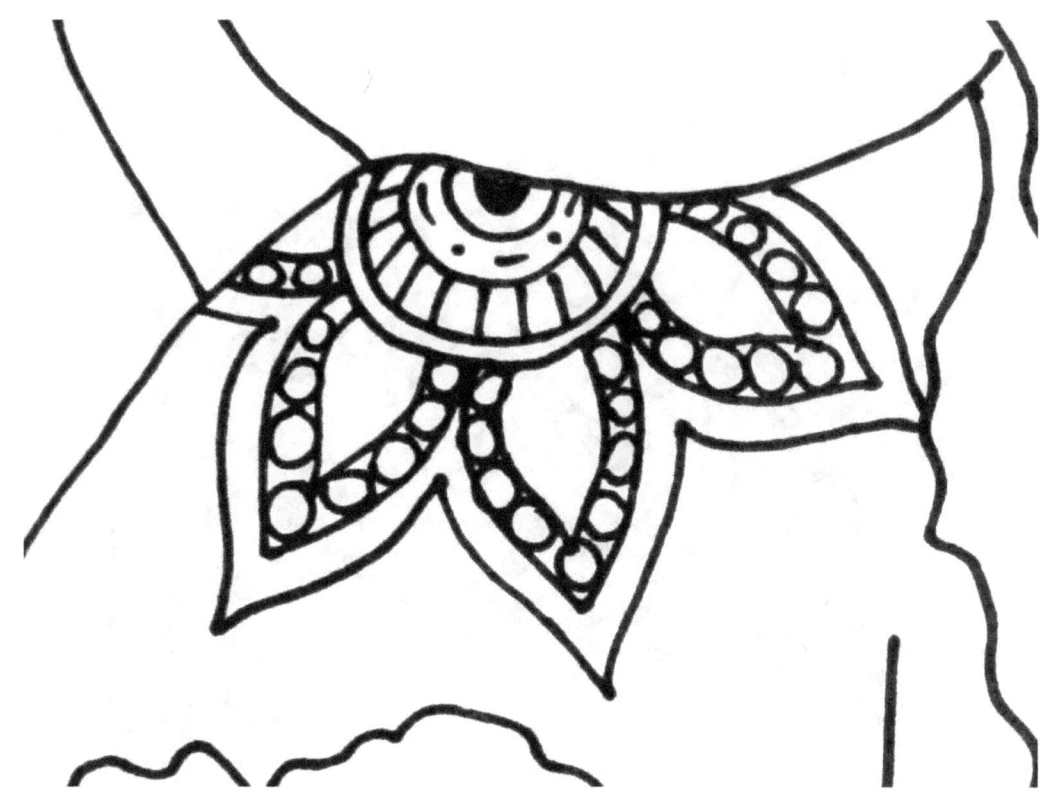

Let`s see what is the next thing that will be a playground for our creativity! Well, we are just going to expand the flower pattern on a doodle dog`s back as displayed on a picture below. This is extremely nice Zen doodle pattern. It looks like a flower goes into the fish scales. Right drawing shows how you can precede this beautiful Zen pattern on one of the hind legs of a beagle and his tail, into something completely different, but equally interesting.

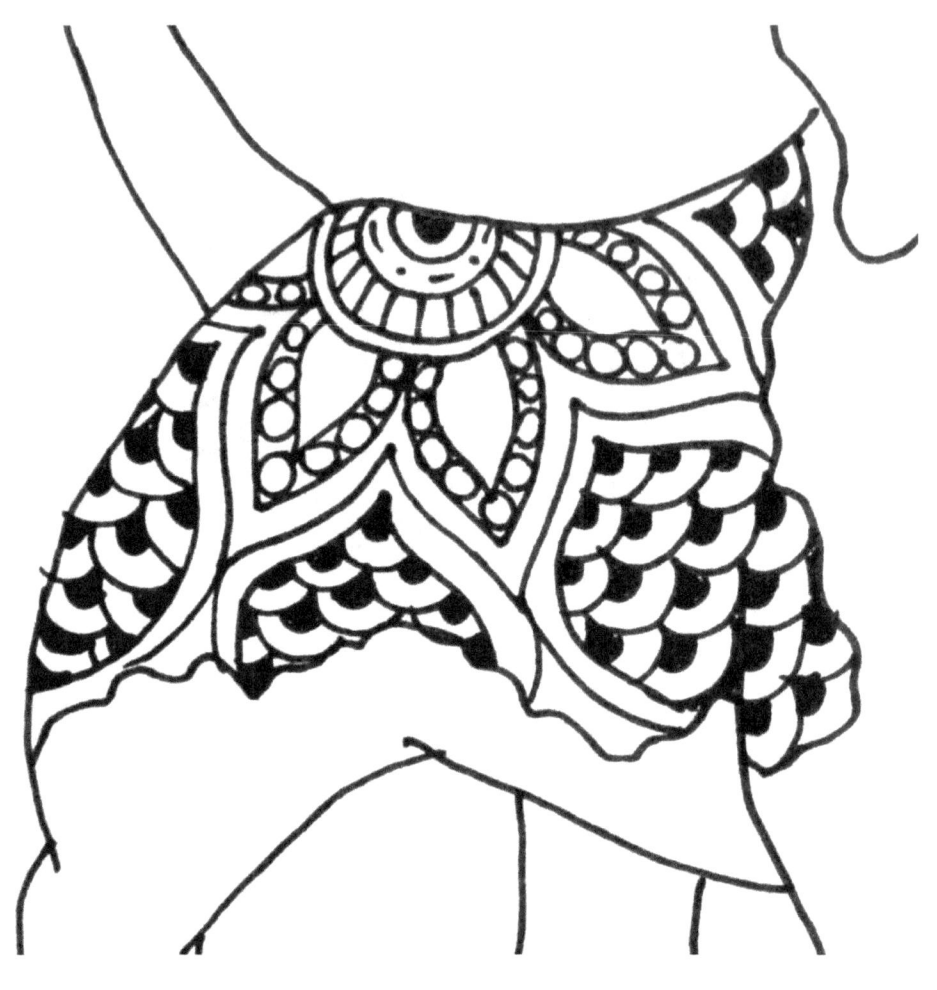

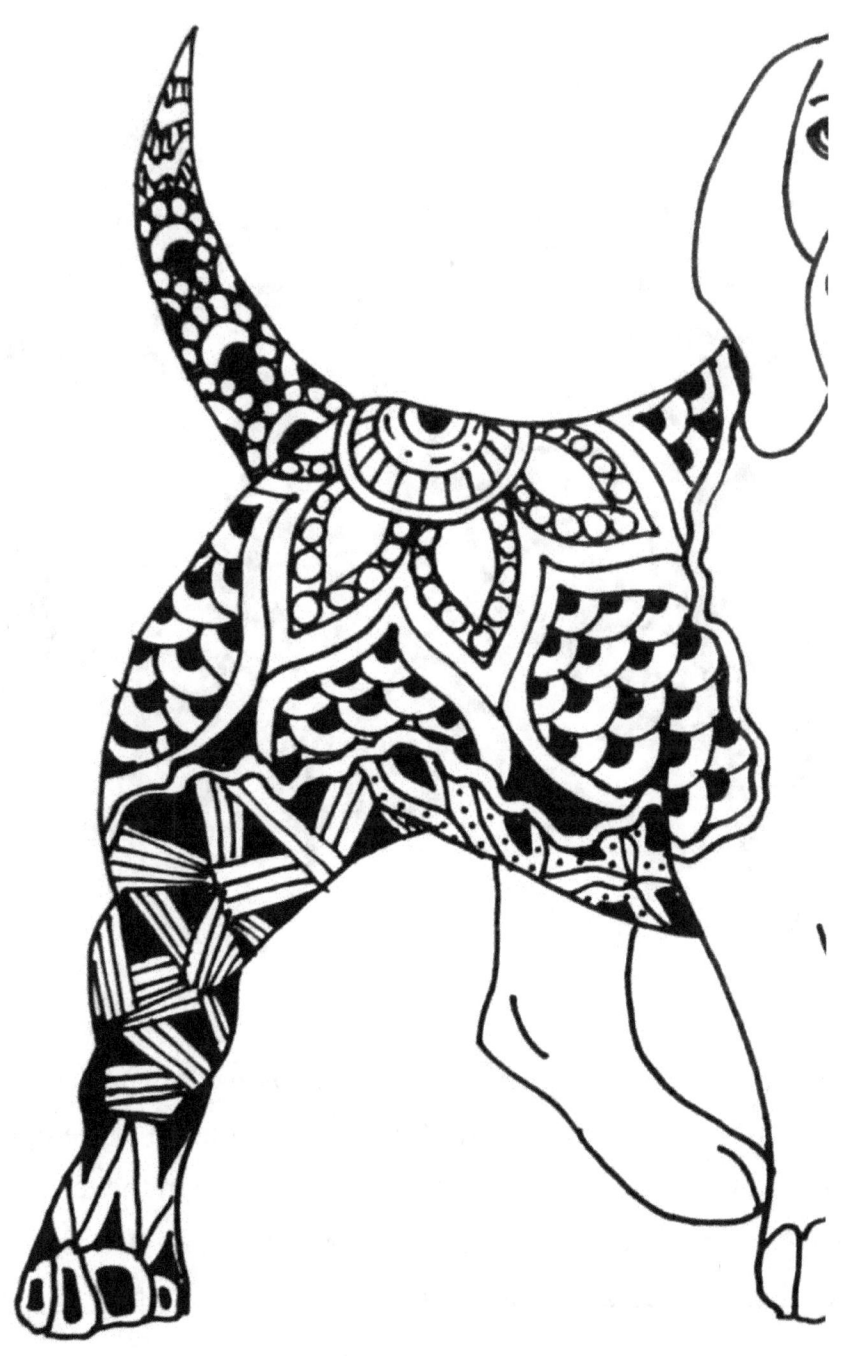

We will now move on to his cute ears and draw various semicircles on them as you can closely see in a drawing below that shows his head.

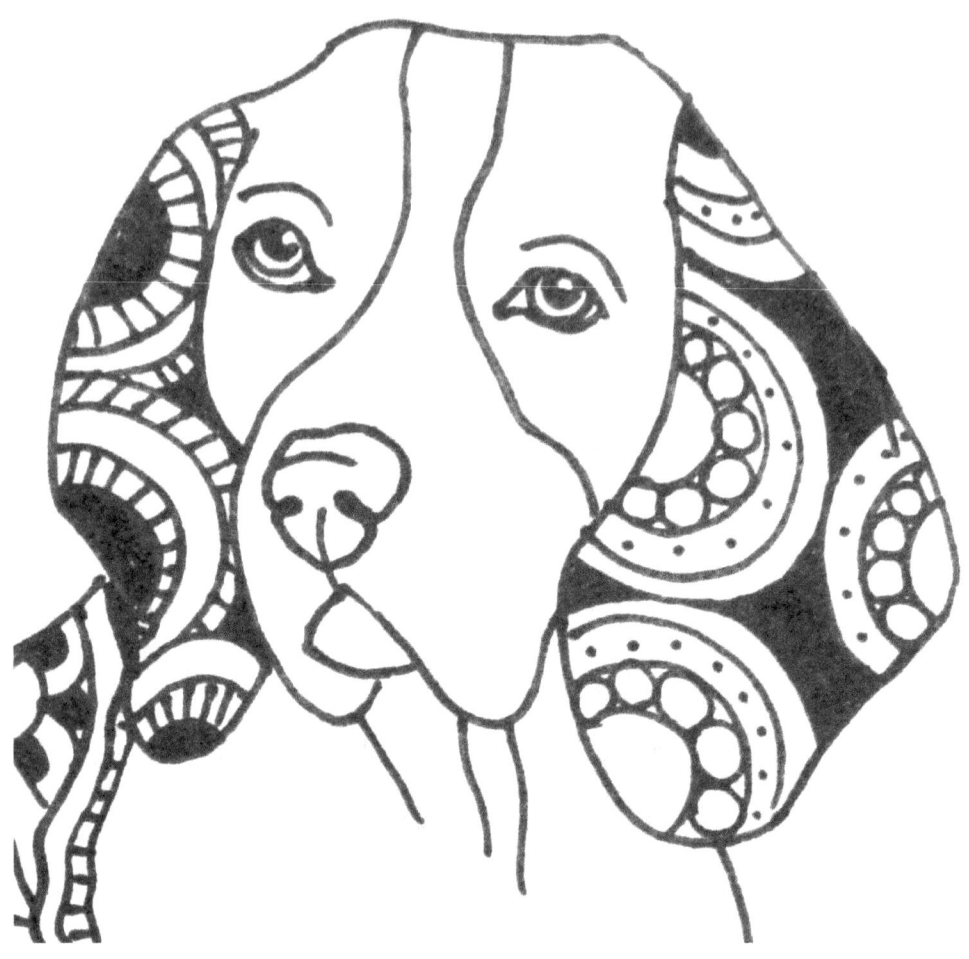

The following picture shows the next steps in drawing Zen doodle beagle. The first thing that will surely attract your attention is the upper part of the front leg where there is a very interesting pattern in the form of a snail shell. In the middle of beagle`s chest is a big star, whose two branches you can`t see all the way because they are obscured by the front legs.

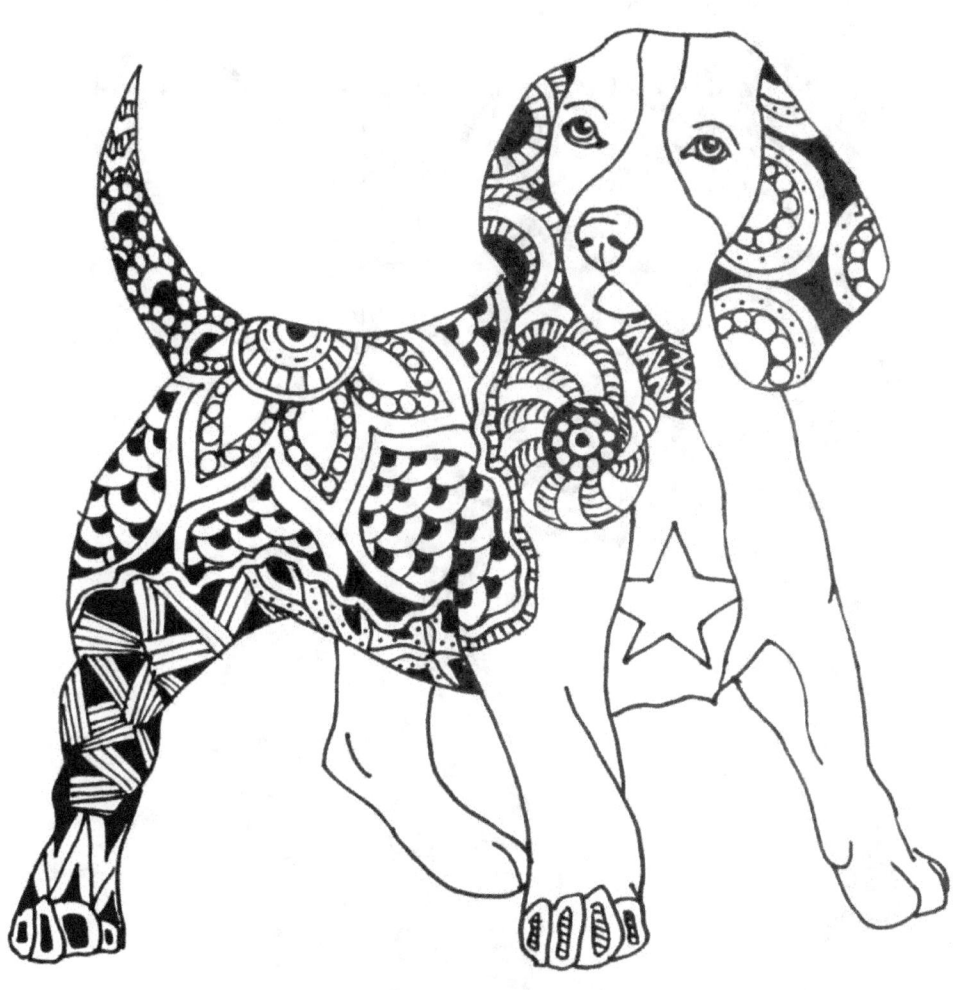

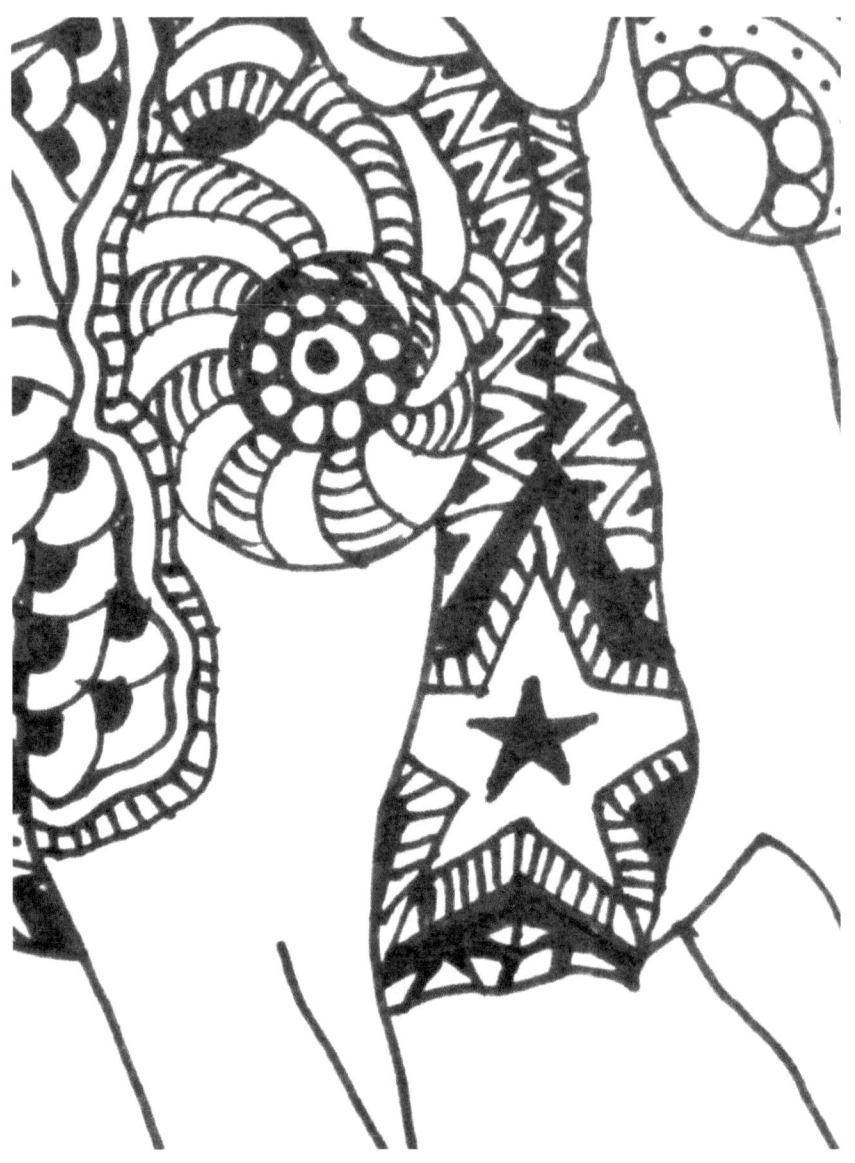

We will now fill out his whole chest with a Zen doodle that is zoomed on the picture on the left.

Next we will decorate the beagle`s right front leg. On the first drawing below you can see a zoomed right leg, and on the second picture the whole drawing as it should be so far.

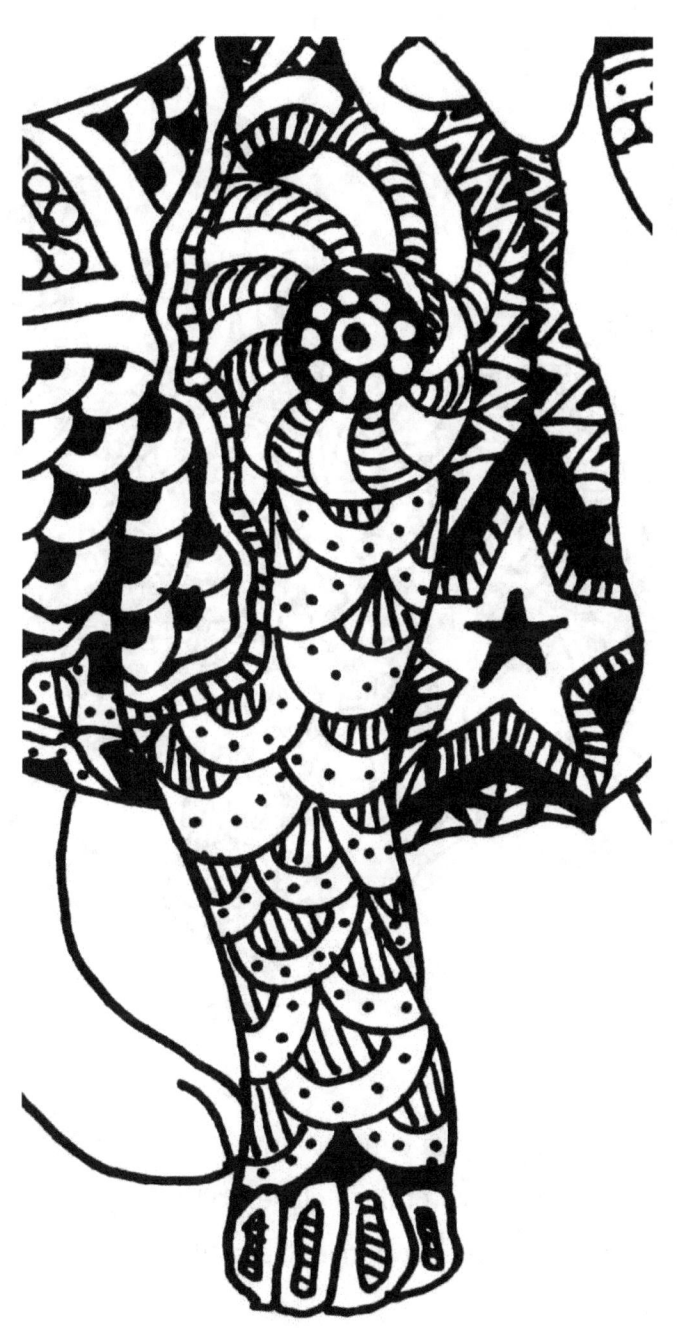

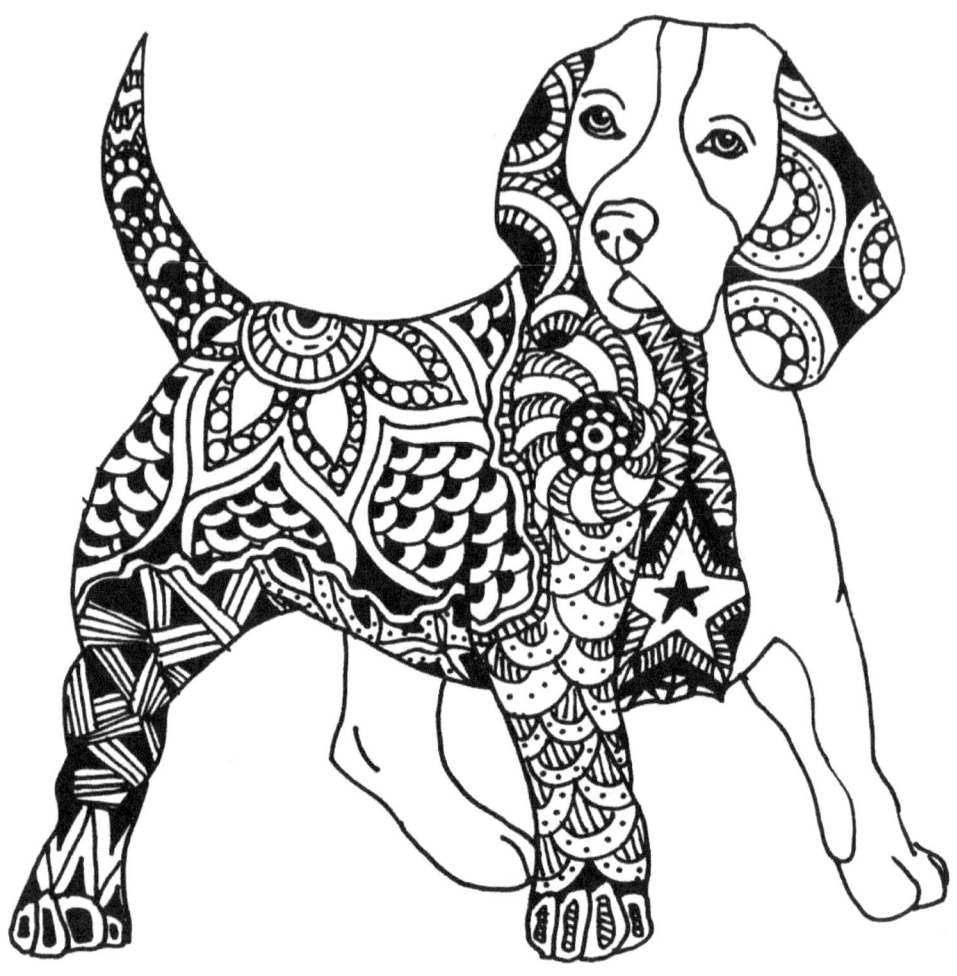

On the next drawing below you can see how to fill in the front left and the front back leg of a beagle. If you take a closer look, you will see that his front leg is divided in two different sections. The drawing is deliberately large in order to ease the job for you.

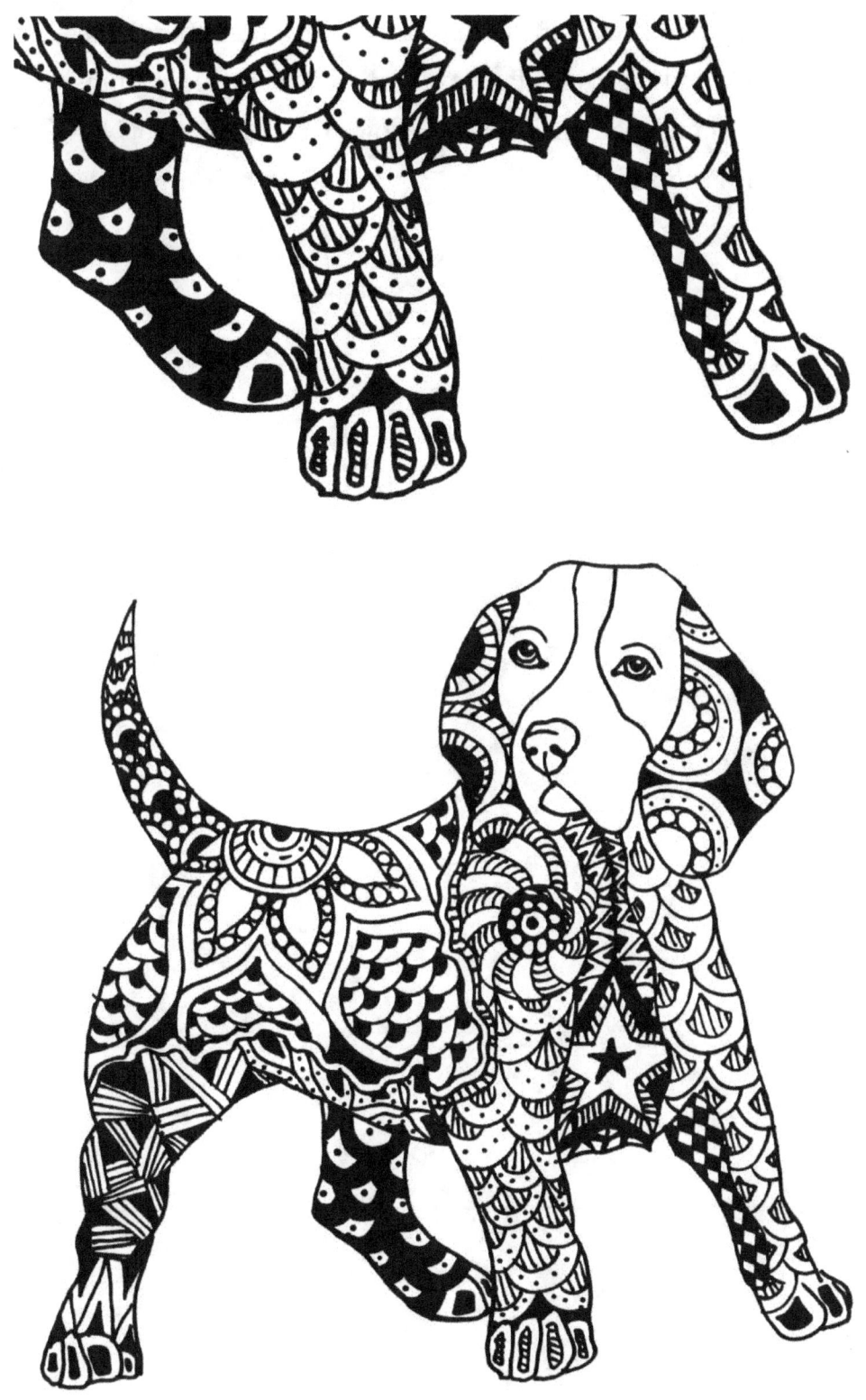

There is only one thing left for us to draw in order to complete our Zen doodle beagle and that is his face. You can take a close look of his snout and the parts around it on the picture below. I sure hope you have enjoyed drawing this beautiful dog!

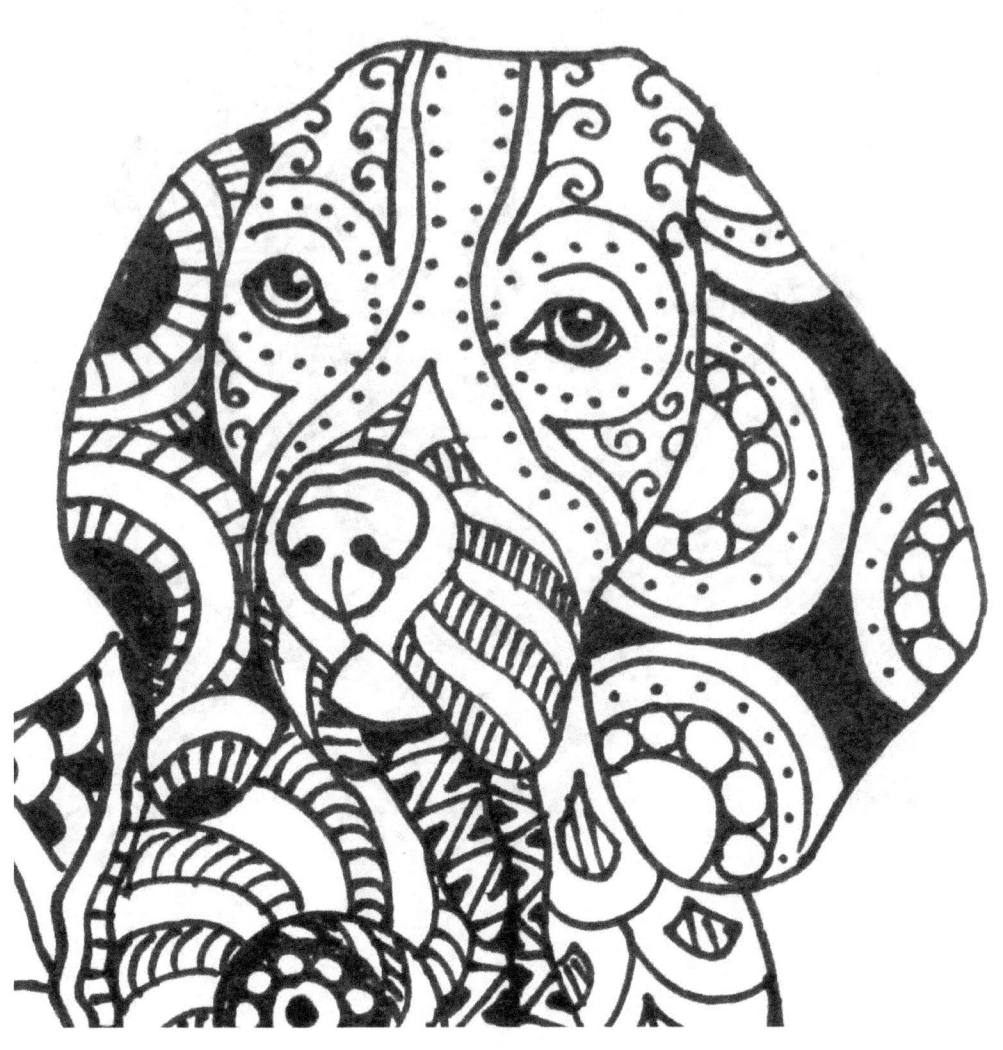

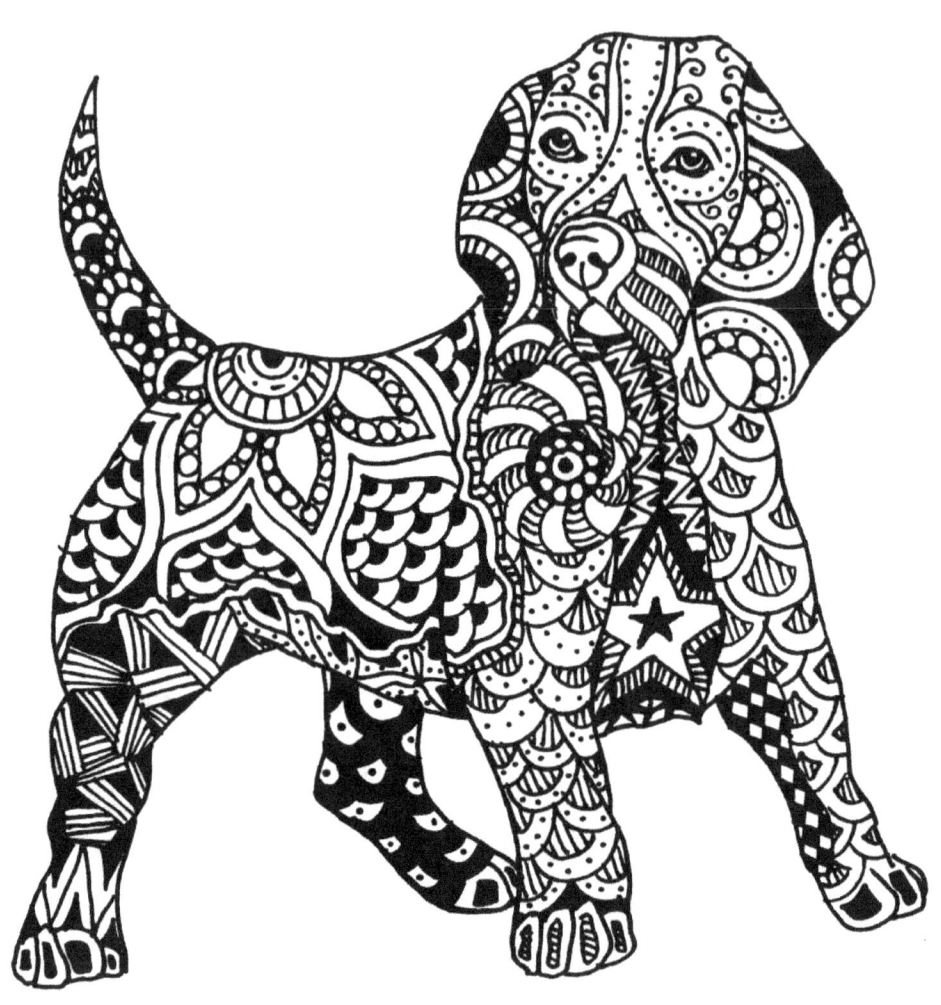

Chapter 6- Zen Bulldog

Lovers of "dangerous" dogs would say that we have saved the best for last! Although today's bulldog descended from its aggressive ancestors, he eventually became a beautiful dog with a good nature. He is a faithful companion, a noble, strong, brave and a proud dog. Friendly look and the similar character make it the perfect pet, especially for families with children or other pets. Bulldog generates a very strong bond with its owner, and sometimes he does not even want to go out into the yard without him. They are not very active and do not be surprised if you have to drag or carry him to the house. Their nice look and wrinkled skin attract attention; the whole park will want to pet him. So, we'll draw his very distinctive head. Pay attention to creases in the drawing below.

You have to be very patient to catch all those wrinkles on bulldog`s face, especially around his snout, as well as his small ears and drooping eyelids. That`s why you can watch this big drawing below to be sure you are doing it the right way. Again, I will remind you that it is better if you use a lead pencil first.

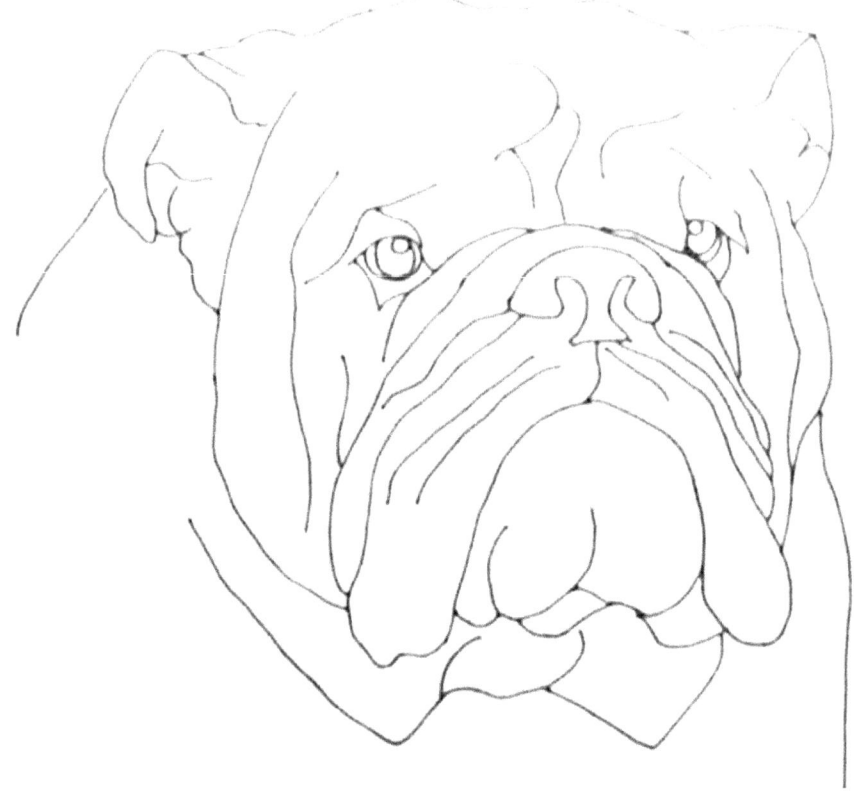

After you have finished this hard work of drawing all those wrinkles, we will move on to the bulldog`s first big wrinkle around his snout. You can see it zoomed on the two drawings below. Don`t forget to paint his eyes with black marker as shown.

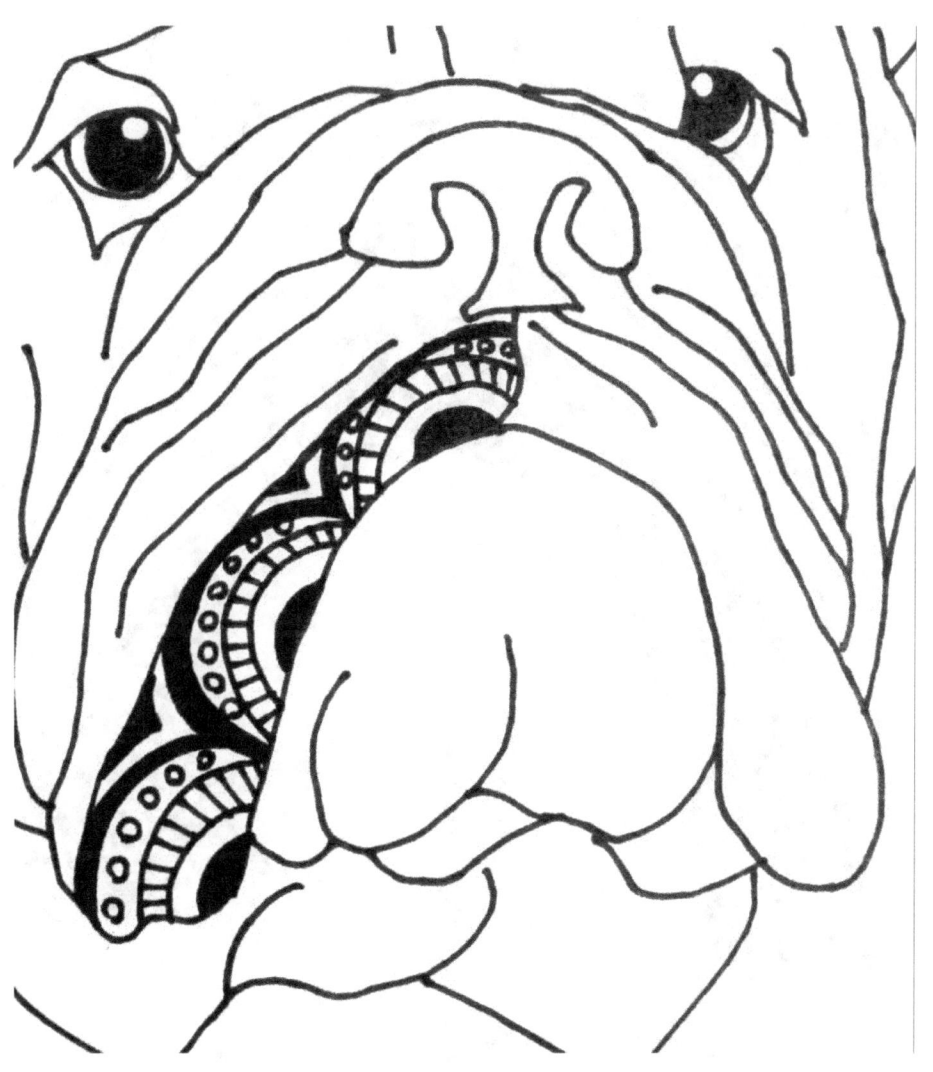

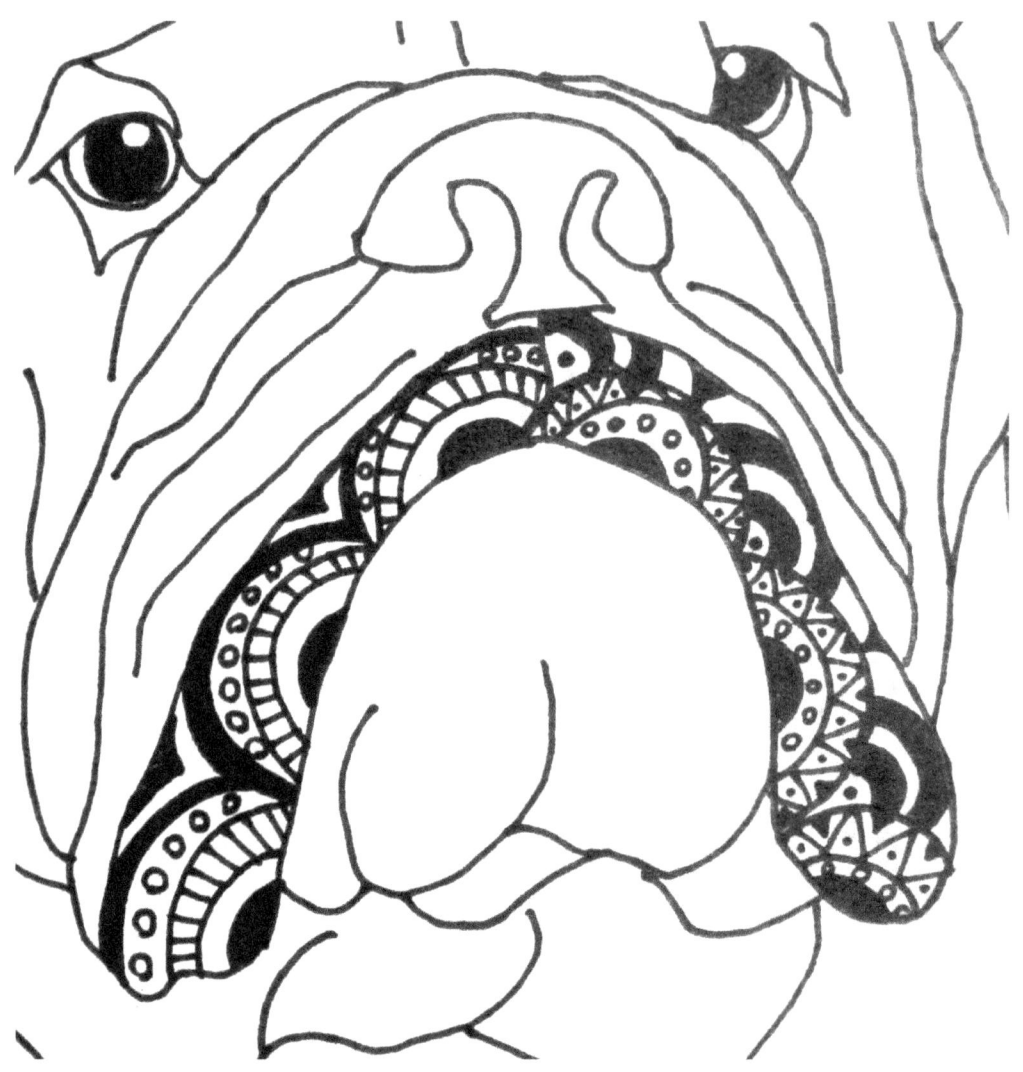

Then, we will just fill his big wrinkles with various Zen doodles as they are some sort of rows. I assume explanations can`t help you much when it comes to this sort of drawings, so keep your eyes on the pictures below.

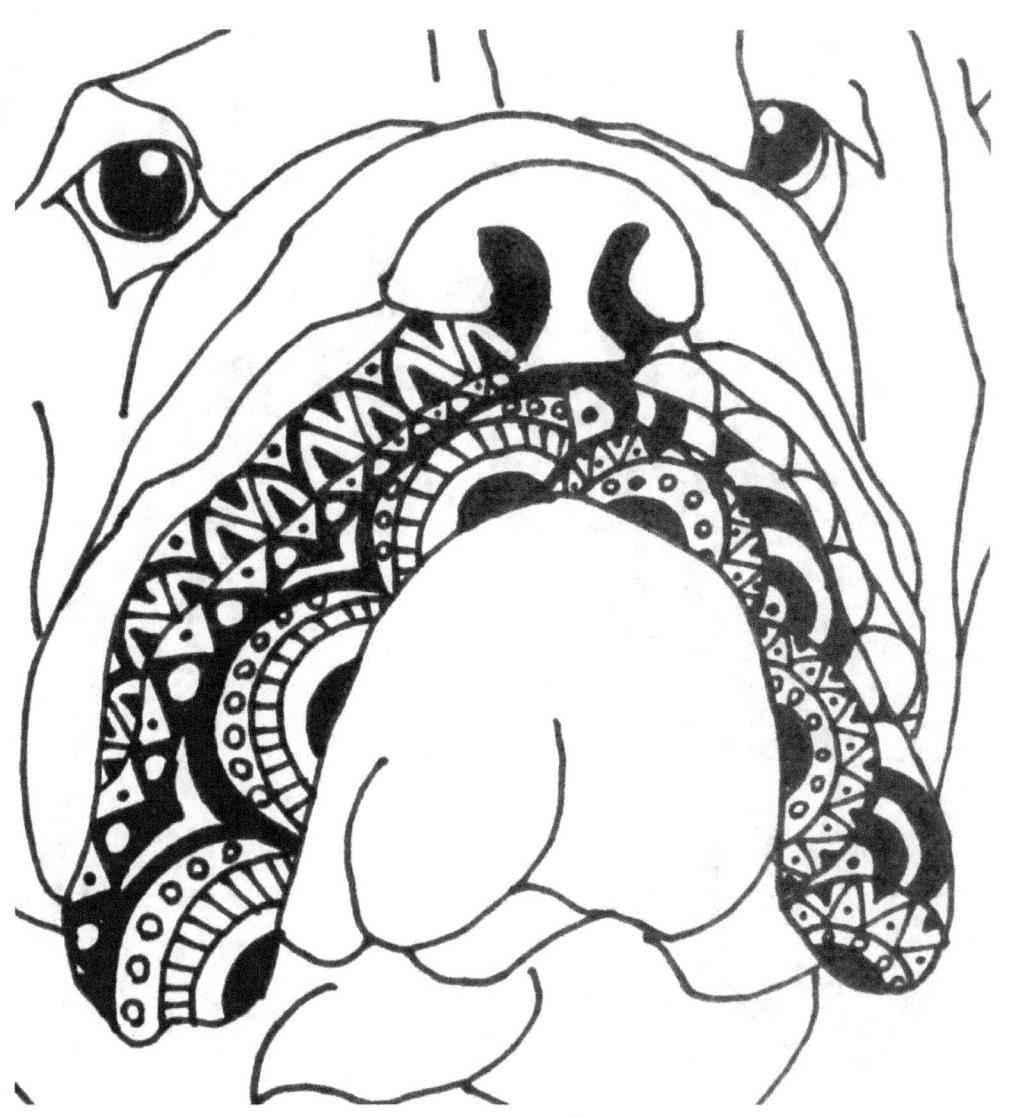

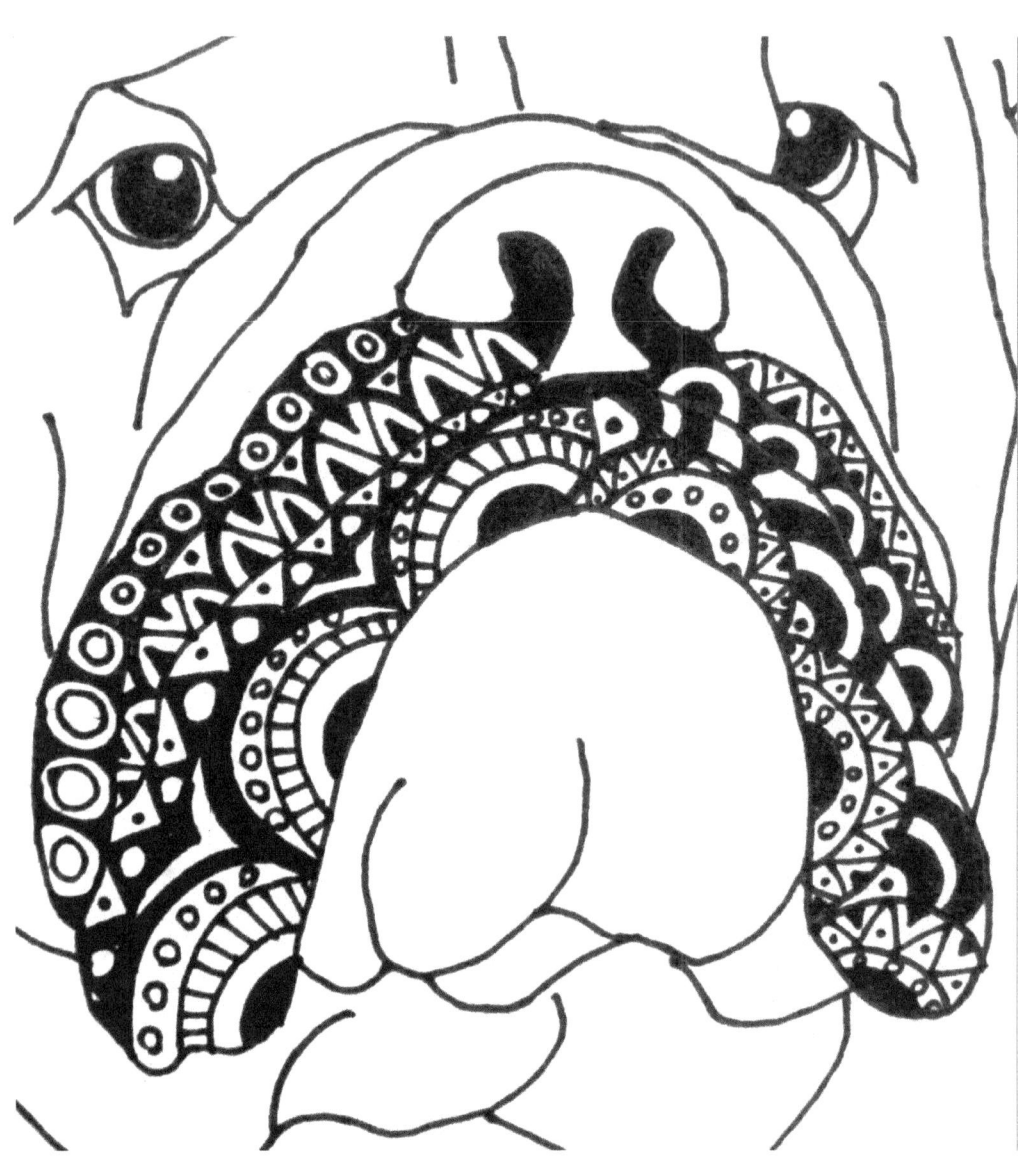

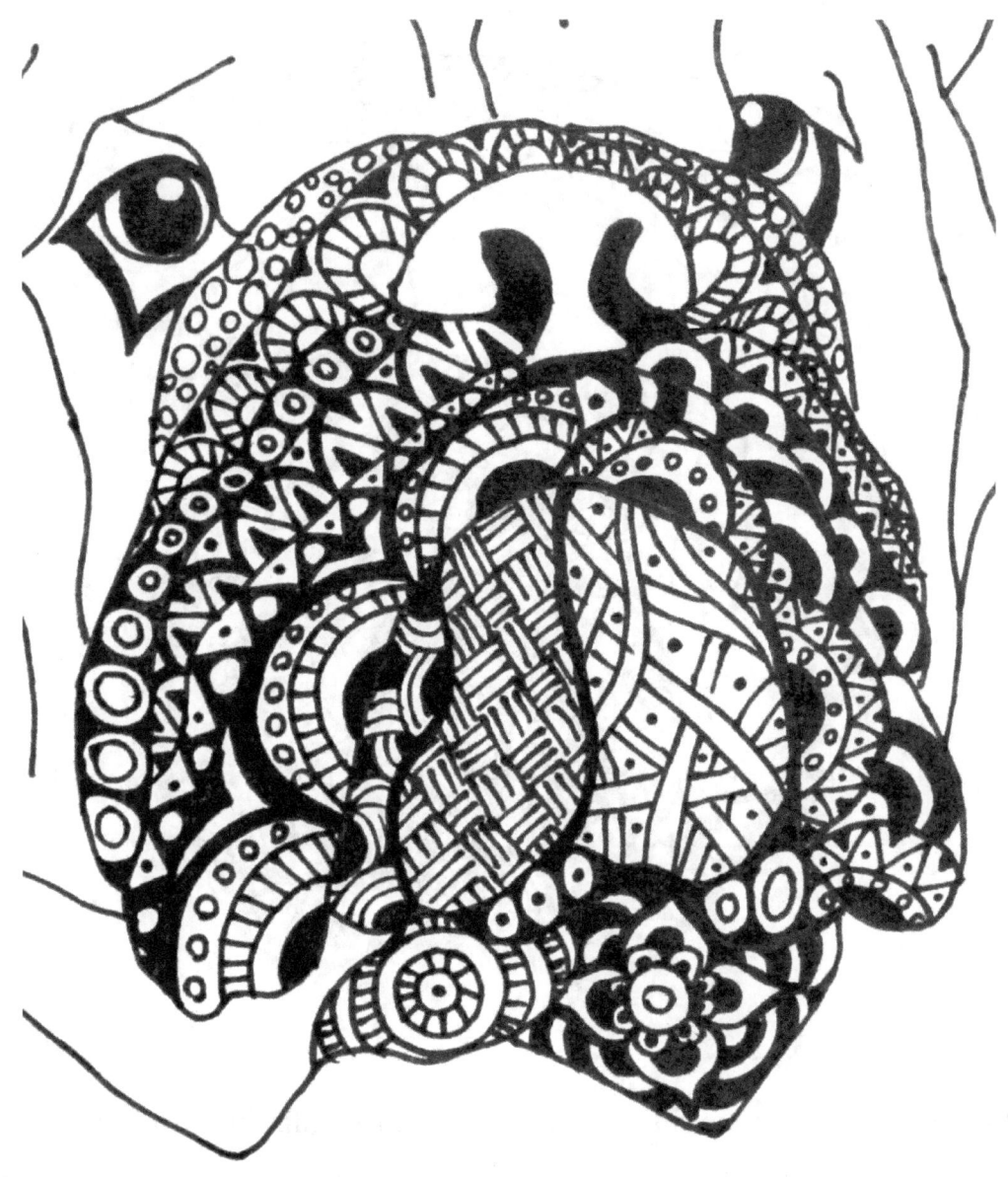

The picture above represents all facial wrinkles and lines on the Bulldog`s face located near his muzzle. I hope you can see it well.

Now, you have to see the whole picture so you can draw his wrinkled neckband around his neck as well as that Zen doodle on the top of his head in a form of leaves. He is getting his Zen art look.

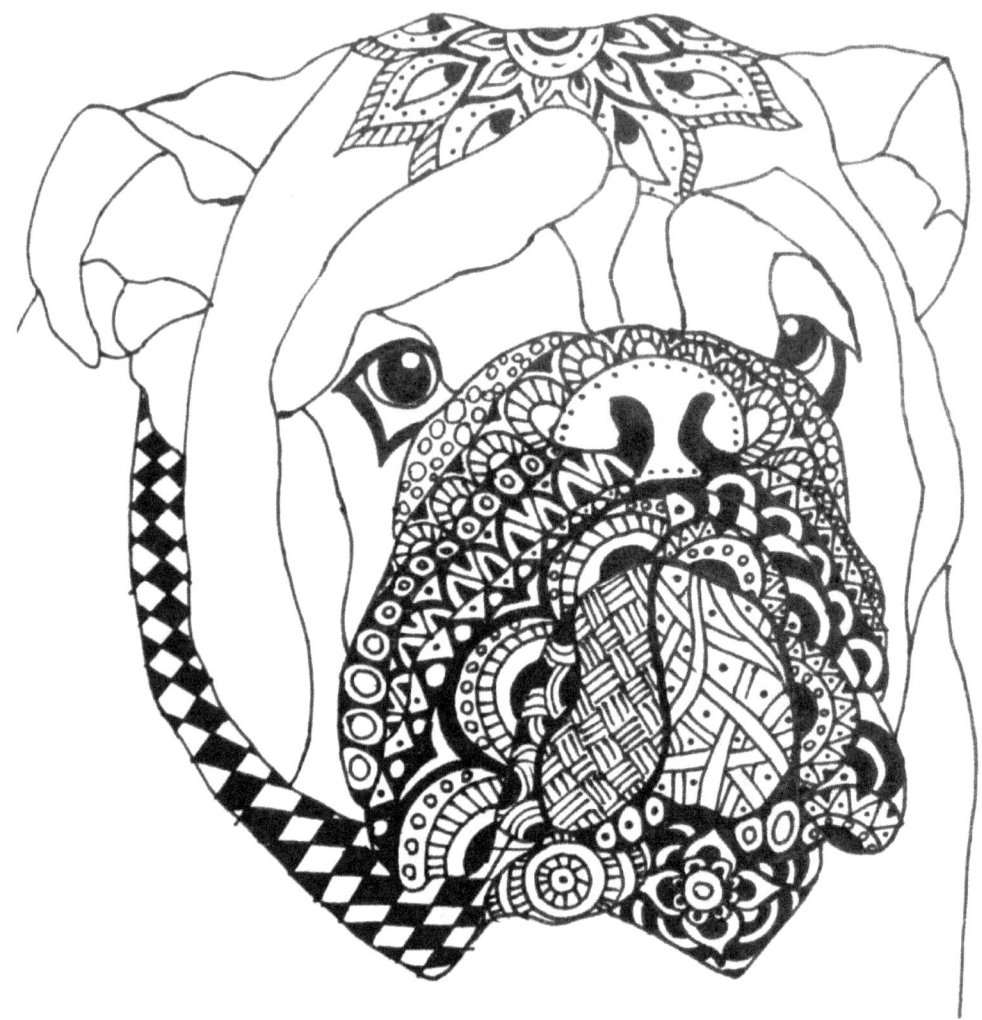

Our next step will be to fill out the rest of his recognizable wrinkles on his face as shown on the large drawings below. You can see a lot of leaf patterns on his face, so focus on that! We can agree that this is the hardest Zen doodle dog in this book, so you might even need a couple of days to finish it.

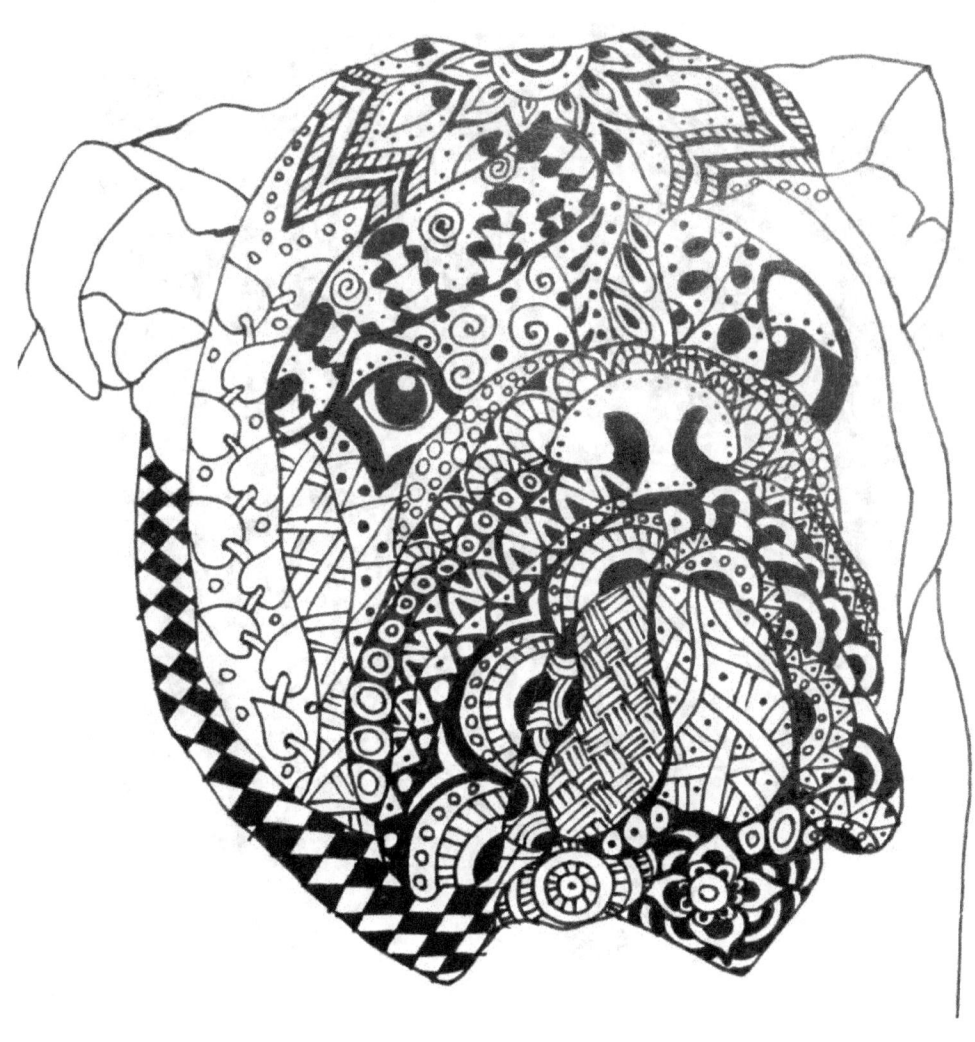

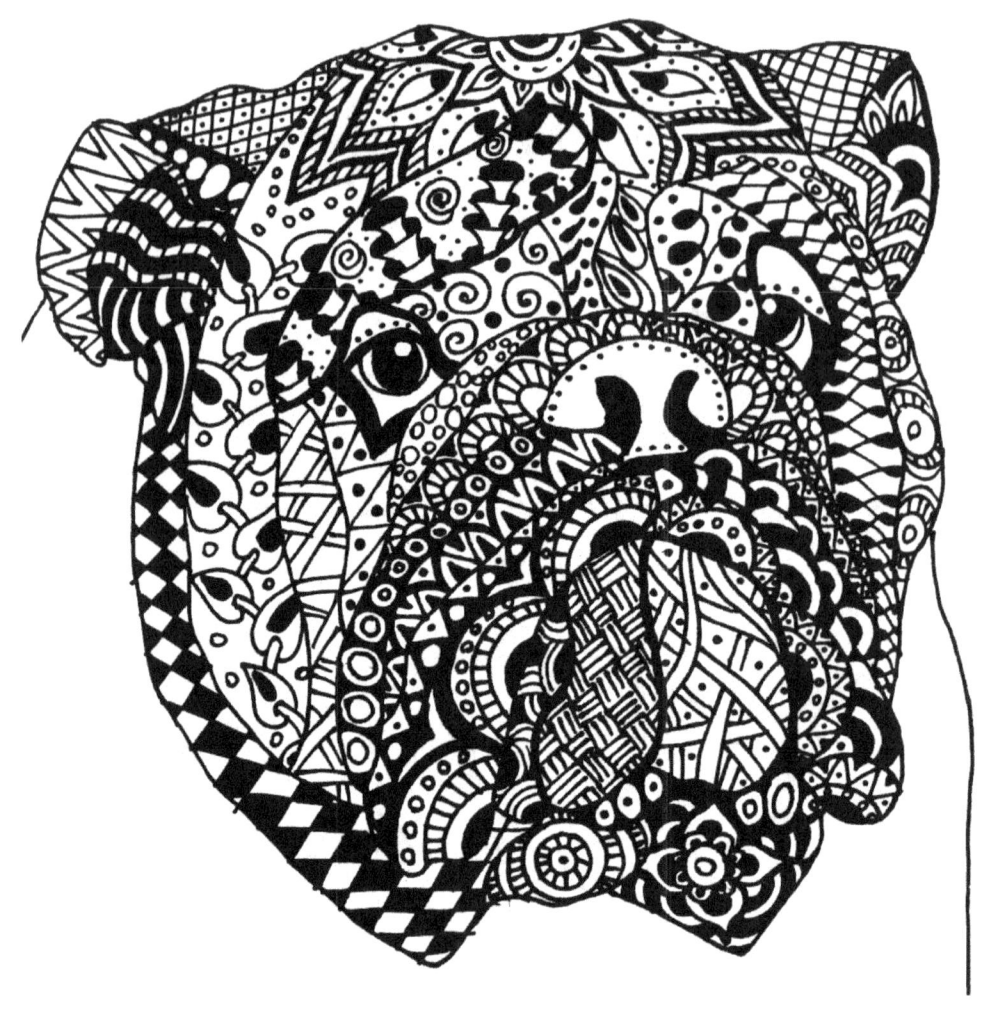

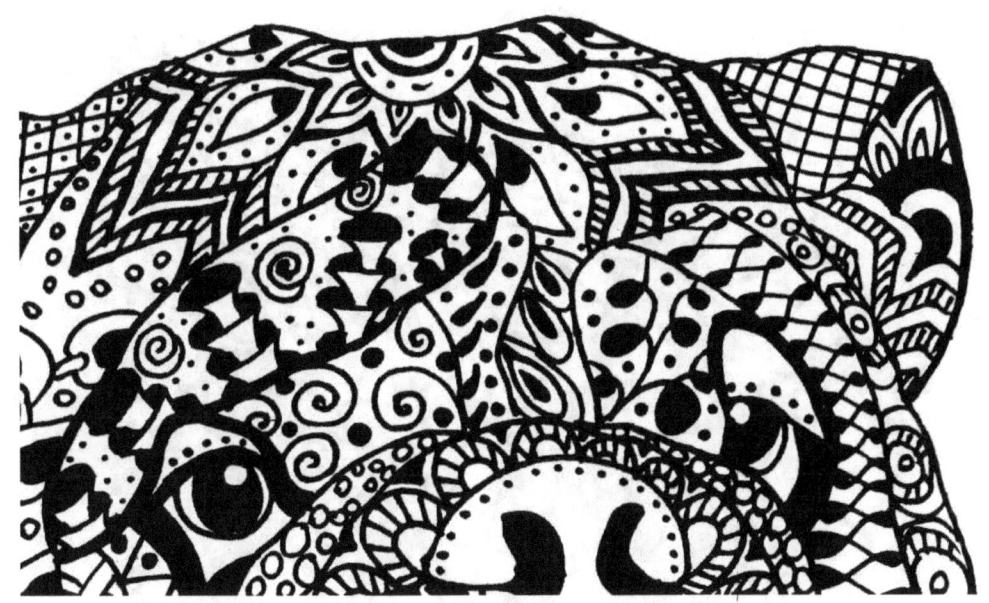

In the last two pictures of bulldog`s head, you can see the final works, which require your full attention and concentration. Zen bulldog would be a good tattoo, but only if a true artist decides to draw it.

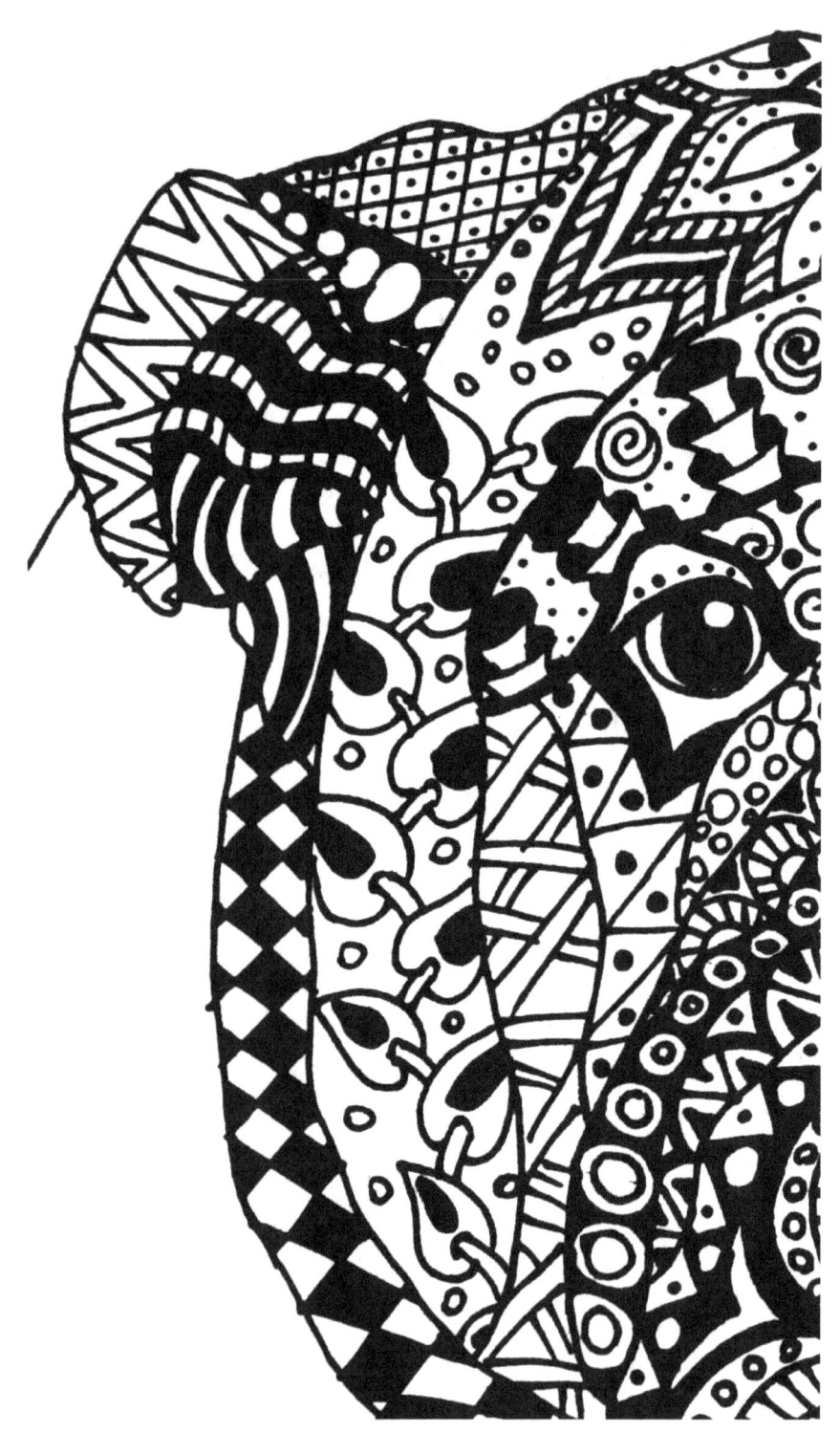

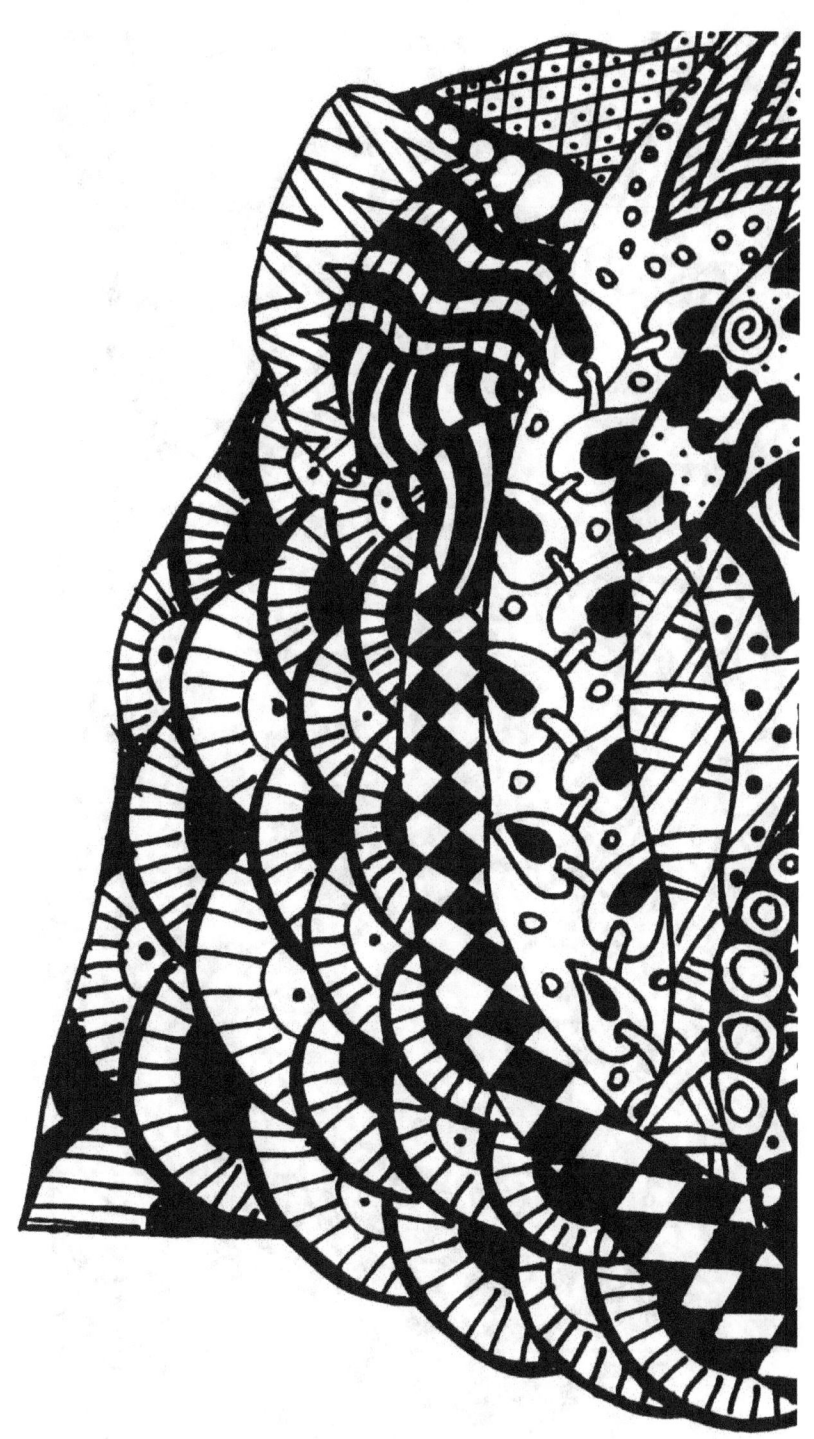

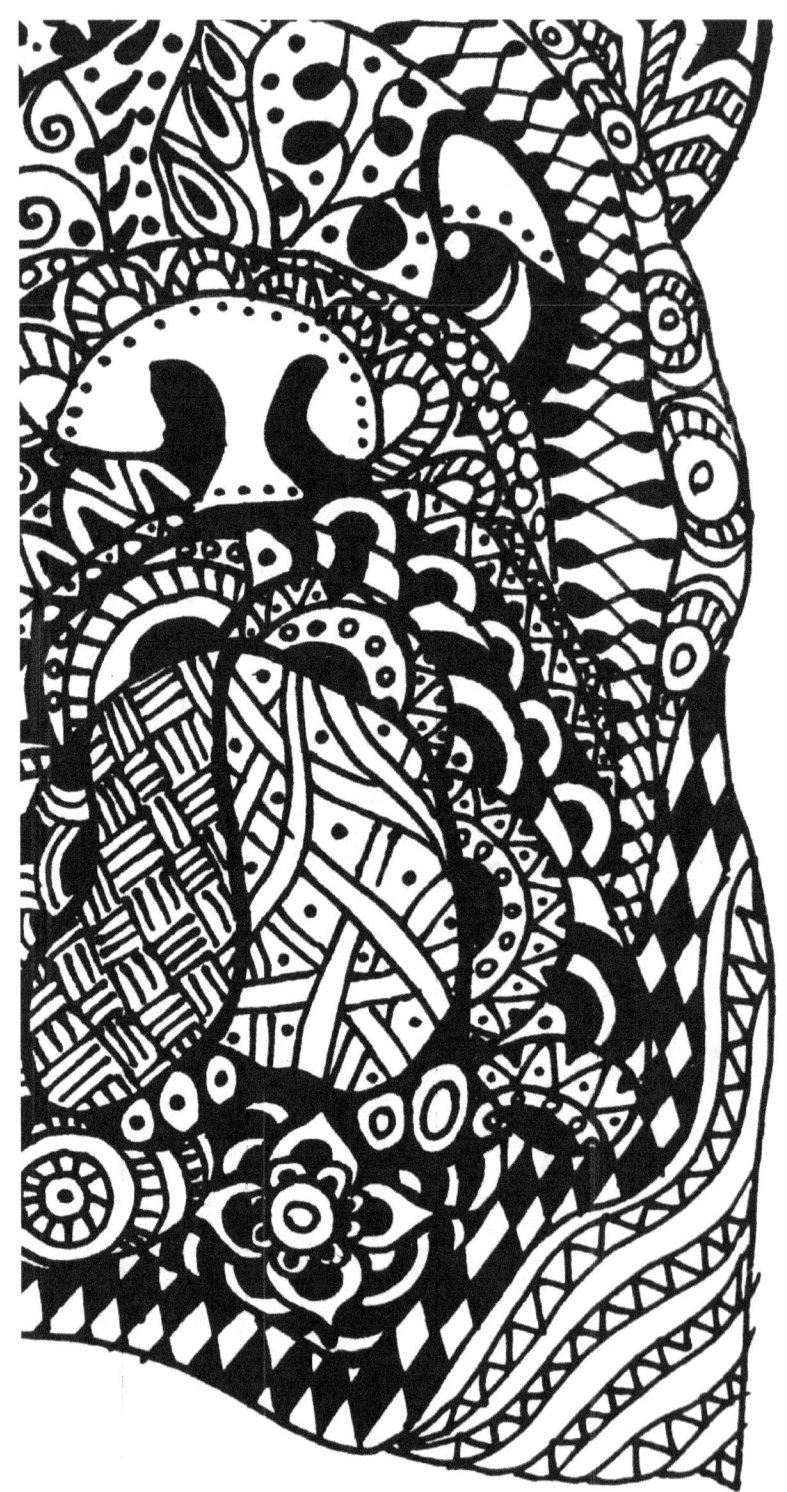

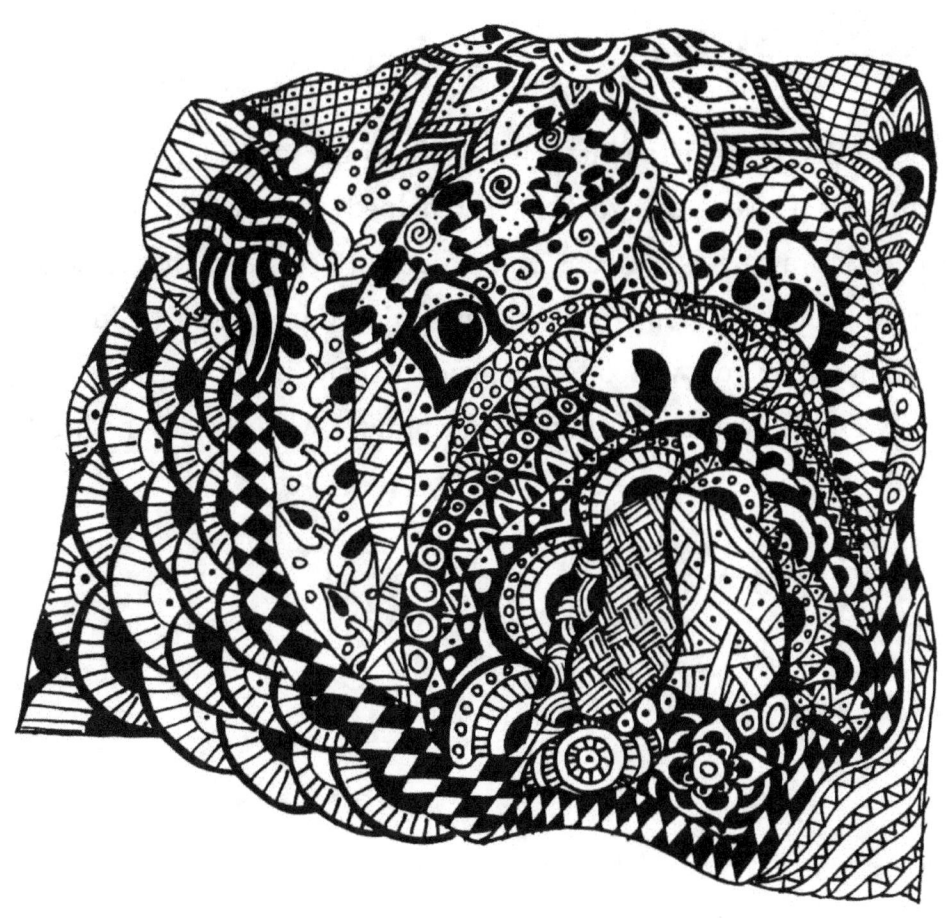

Conclusion

The book, "Zen Dogs: Drawing Zen Doodle Dogs" was created primarily to entertain, but if beside this goal she also helped you understand the welfare of Zen art of drawing as a means of meditation, I consider that to be a great advantage. I sincerely hope that you have enjoyed in these six Zen drawings of dogs and that you will often return to them if you feel the need to creatively express yourself or purify your mind. I wish you all the best! Stay in a Zen!

Thank you!

Thank you for choosing our book, we hope you found it interesting and helpful.

If you liked the book, please give us a favor to write your review.

We would really appreciate this!

If you would like to have a bonus – **FREE BOOK**, please send the screenshot of your review to this e-mail: **kelly.artbooks@gmail.com** and we will send you **a FREE BOOK** in PDF as a **GIFT!****

Hope to see you in our future books and good luck in your drawing experience!

** in the e-mail subject please mention the name of the book you reviewed and the author.

Other Books from Jane McKenty

ZEN DOODLE: The Art of Zen Doodle. Drawing Guide with Step by Step Instructions. Book one.

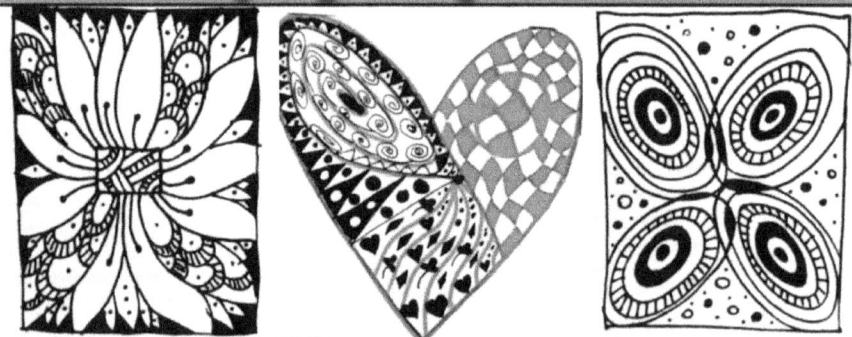

ZEN Doodle: The Art of Zen Drawing. Master Zen Doodle with Step by Step Instructions. Book two.

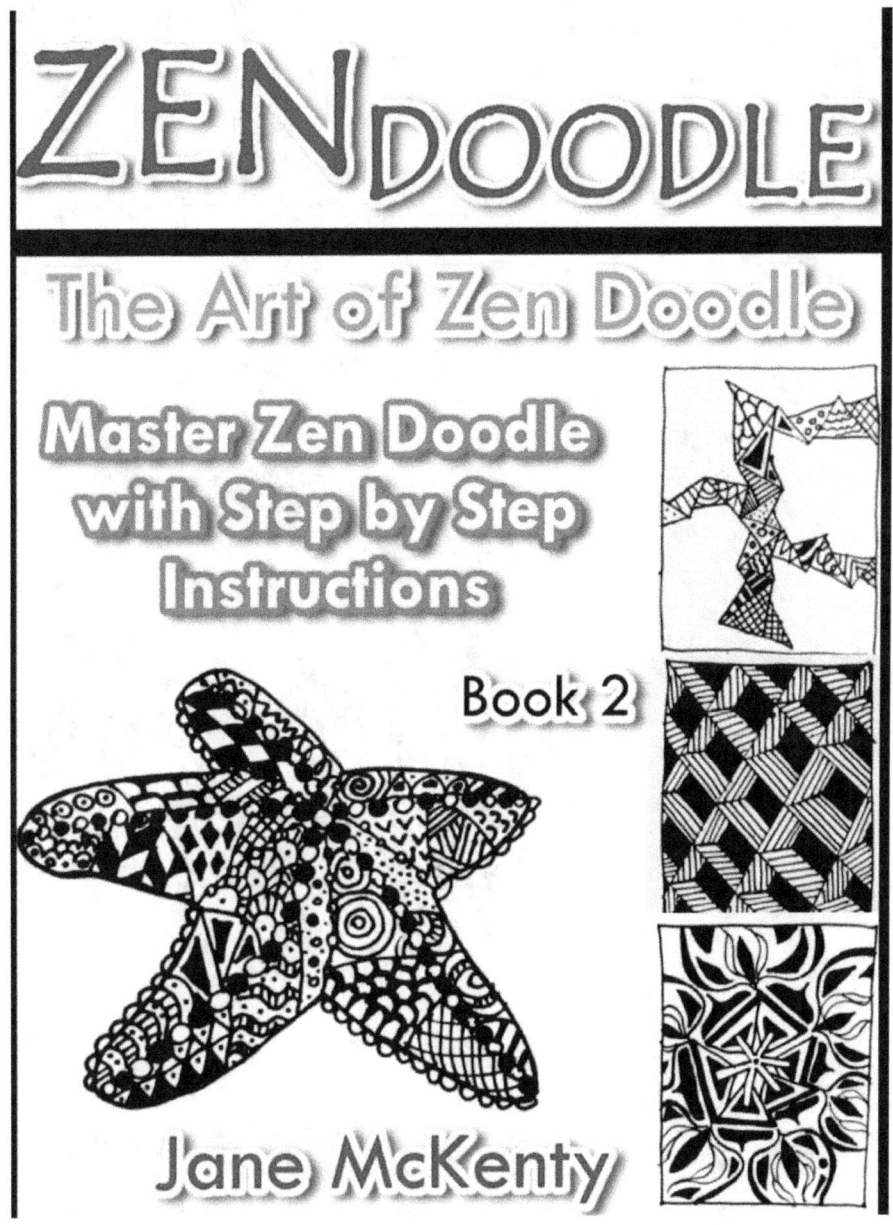

ZEN CATS: Drawing Amazing Zen Doodle Cats

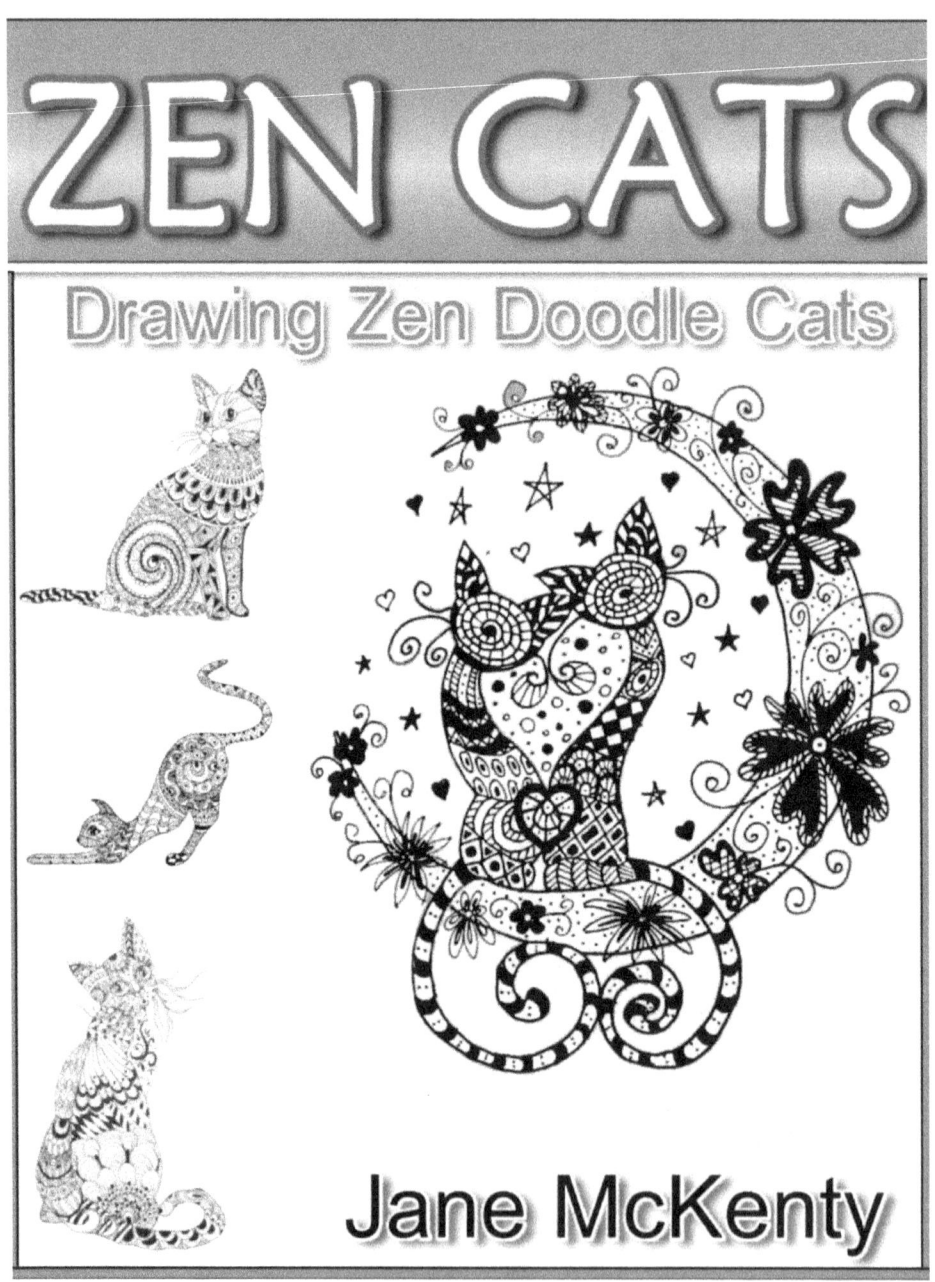

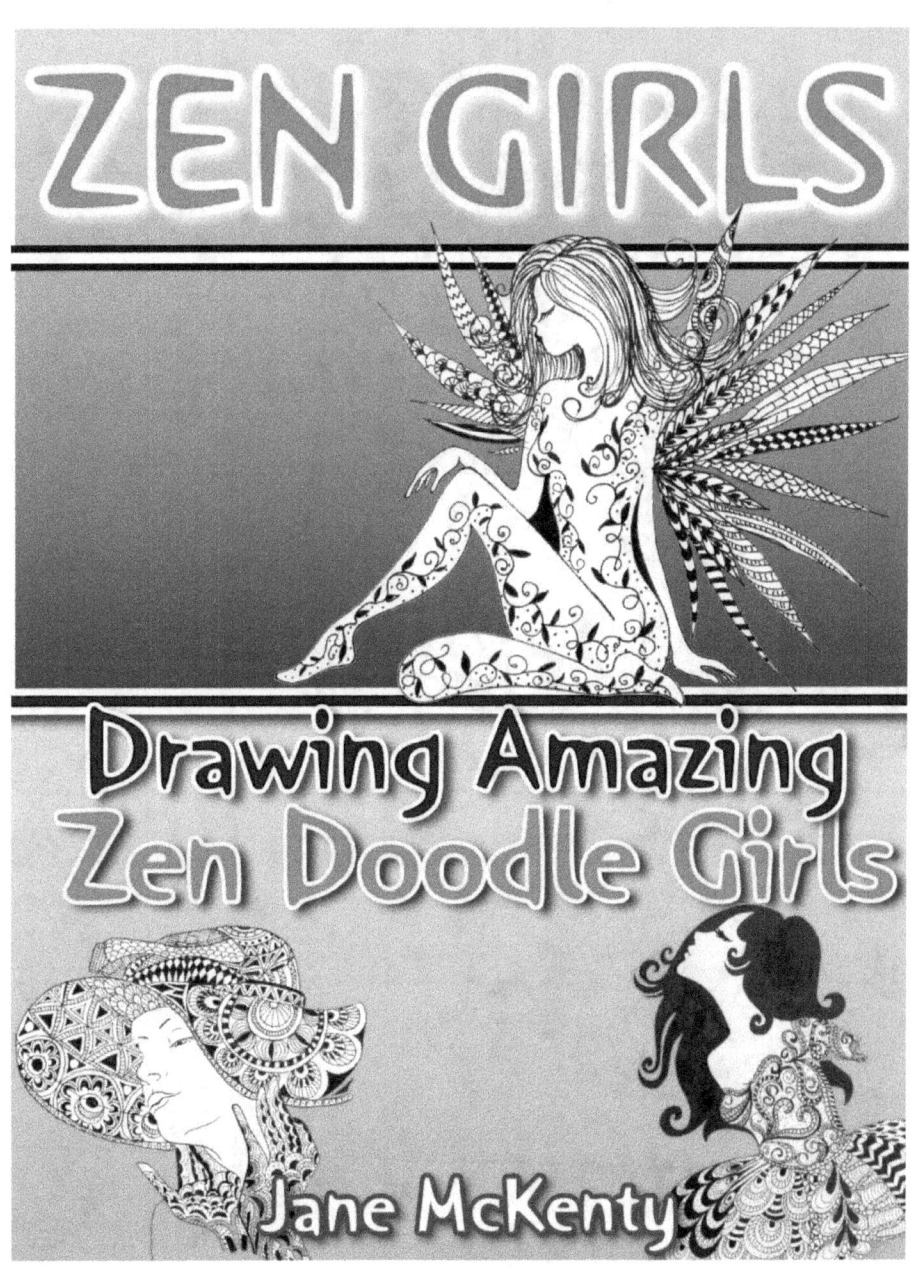

ZEN Horses: Drawing Amazing Zen Doodle Horses!

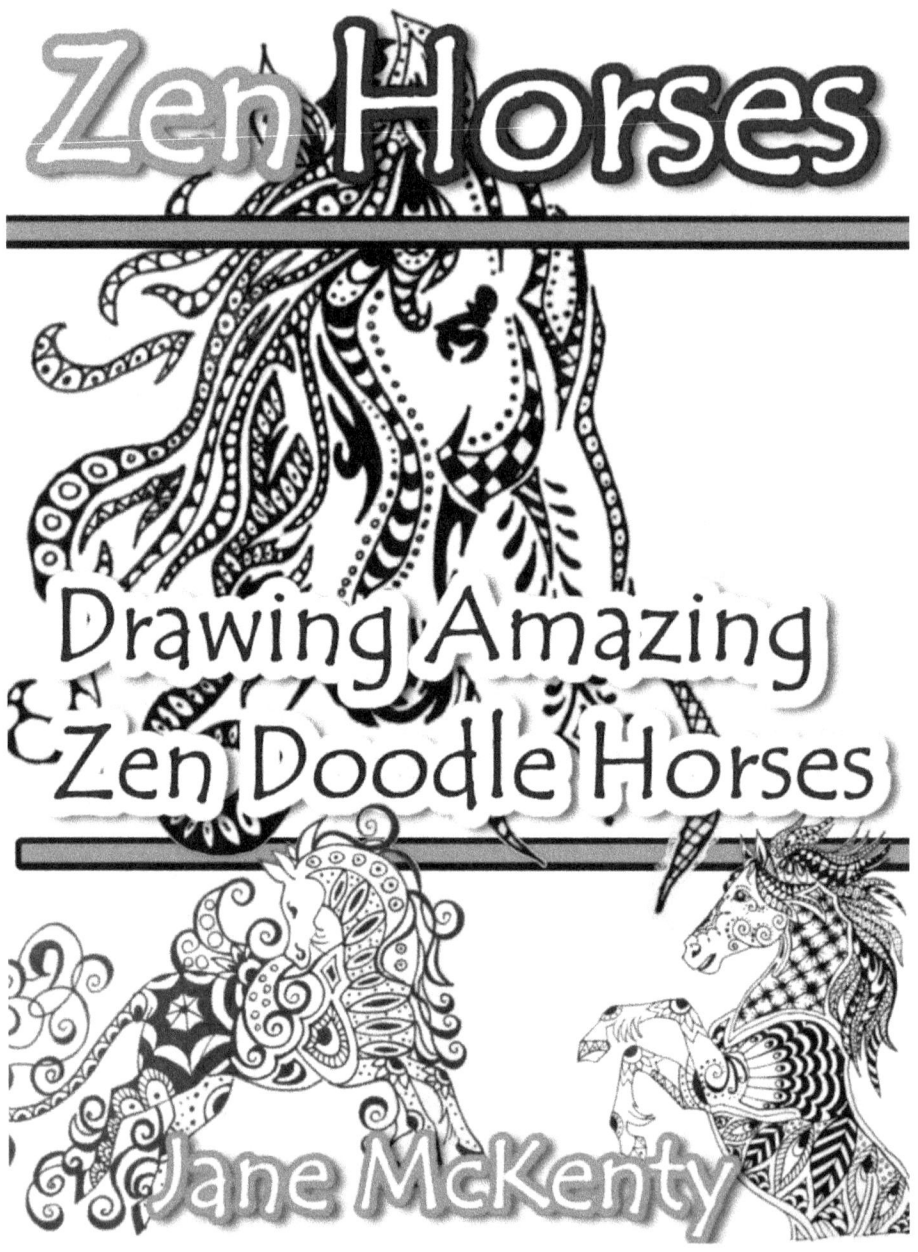

ZEN Doodle Art: Drawing Underwater Life with Amazing Zen Doodle Technique

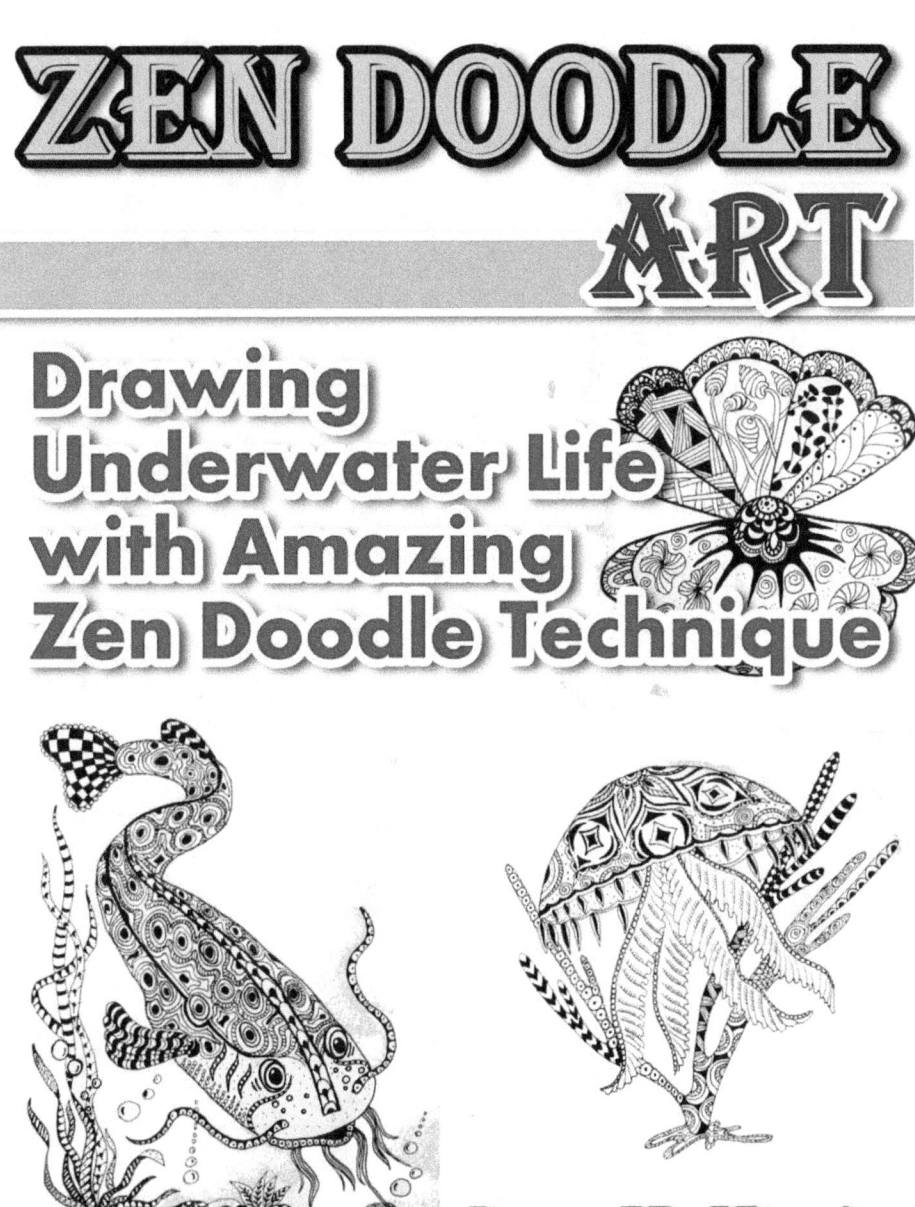